Metabolic Confusion Diet Cookbook for Endomorph Women Over 50

A Complete Recipe Collection Built on the New A.D.A.P.T.I.V.E. System to Burn Fat, Balance Hormones & Feel Energized in Less Than 28 Days

By

Emma Grace Stanton

Disclaimer

This book is intended for informational and educational purposes only and should not be considered as medical advice. The content is based on the author's research, experiences, and opinions, and it is designed to support, not replace, the relationship that exists between a reader and their healthcare provider. Always consult with a qualified healthcare professional before beginning any new diet, exercise program, or lifestyle changes, especially if you have pre-existing medical conditions.

While every effort has been made to ensure the accuracy of the information contained in this book, the author and publisher assume no responsibility for errors, omissions, or contrary interpretations of the subject matter herein. The author and publisher are not responsible for any health issues or injuries that may arise from following the information provided in this book.

Individual results may vary, and no guarantee of specific outcomes is made. The reader assumes full responsibility for their health decisions and the application of any recommendations provided in this book.

Trademarks

All trademarks, service marks, and trade names mentioned in this book are the property of their respective owners. Use of these trademarks does not imply any affiliation or endorsement.

Legal Notice

This book is sold with the understanding that neither the author nor the publisher is engaged in rendering legal, financial, medical, or other professional advice. If expert assistance is required, the services of a competent professional should be sought. Any perceived slights of specific individuals, organizations, or products are unintentional.

Table Of Contents

- Emotional Eating and Its Secret Triggers—And How to Break Free.

Part Two: The A.D.A.P.T.I.V.E. Metabolic System

5. The A.D.A.P.T.I.V.E. System Explained

- The 8 Core Pillars to Reset and Recharge Your Metabolism.
- Why Adaptability Is the Secret to Success.
- How to Work With Your Body, Not Against It.

6. A: Active Metabolic Fluctuation

- The 3-Phase Plan to Keep Your Body Guessing and Burning Fat.
- How to Rotate Macronutrients Without Feeling Deprived.
- The Secret to Supercharging Fat Loss While Sleeping.

7. D: Dietary Freedom Through Structure

- The 4 Food Rules That Make Eating Simple.
- How to Build Balanced Meals in Under 10 Minutes.
- Why You Can—and Should—Enjoy Carbs Without Guilt.

8. A: Age-Specific Hormonal Balancing

- The 5 Superfoods for Post-Menopausal Women.
- Foods That Boost Estrogen, Reduce Cortisol, and Stabilize Insulin.
- Daily Rituals to Keep Hormones in Check.

9. P: Personalized Meal Planning Made Easy

- The 3-Step Method to Design Meals for Your Goals.
- Meal Timing for Maximum Energy and Recovery.
- Adapting Your Plan to Real-Life Challenges.

10. T: Tactical Stress Management

- Quick Techniques to Lower Cortisol in 10 Minutes.

Preface

Have you ever stood in front of the mirror and wondered, *When did I stop recognizing myself?* It's not just the reflection that looks different; it's the way you feel—tired, stuck, and unsure of where to even begin. If you've felt this way, I want you to know something important: you're not alone, and this isn't the end of your story.

I remember the day it hit me. I was turning 52, and instead of celebrating, **I felt defeated**. None of the diets I'd tried seemed to work anymore. My body felt heavy, uncooperative, like it had its own agenda that I couldn't control. I was exhausted, not just physically but emotionally, and it felt as though I'd lost a piece of myself along the way. **Sound familiar?**

Here's the truth no one tells you: the problem isn't you. The problem is that **most advice out there wasn't designed for women like us**—women whose bodies are changing, whose lives are full of responsibilities, and who want more than just a number on the scale. We want to feel good again. We want energy, vitality, and confidence.

I don't have a magic solution, and I'll never tell you this will be easy. But what I can tell you is that it's possible. I know because I've been where you are. I've felt the frustration of working so hard and seeing little progress. I've battled the exhaustion that comes from trying to figure it all out on my own. And I've learned that change doesn't happen through deprivation or extreme measures—it happens when you start listening to what your body truly needs and work with it, not against it.

This is also why I made a conscious decision about the format of this book. I wanted it to be more than just practical and motivational—I wanted it to **adapt to your life**. That's why, rather than filling these pages with glossy images of recipes, I've created something more interactive for you. In the book, you'll find a **QR code** that lead to a gallery of **digital recipe images**, accessible anytime from your phone, tablet, or computer. Whether you're meal prepping in the kitchen or scrolling for inspiration, these images are there to guide and motivate you. This approach allowed me to focus these pages on delivering deep insights and practical tools while still providing the visual inspiration you need to stay on track.

This book is about more than just weight loss. It's about **reconnecting with yourself**, reclaiming your energy, and rediscovering what it feels like to truly thrive. Along the way, I'll share what I've learned through my own struggles and through helping others navigate theirs. You'll find practical tools, encouragement, and a roadmap to help you **take that first step**—and the next, and the next.

Thank you for trusting me enough to open these pages. You've already taken a powerful step by choosing to invest in yourself. So take a deep breath, and let's begin this journey together. **The best is yet to come.**

Emma Grace Stanton

Introduction

The Last Health Transformation You'll Ever Need

1. Why You're Not to Blame (and Why This Book Will Finally Work for You)

If you've ever felt like no matter what you try, the weight just won't budge—or worse, it keeps coming back—you're not alone. And more importantly, you're not to blame. The truth is, traditional diets were never designed with your body, age, or unique needs in mind. That's why this book is different. It's not about blaming you for past struggles; it's about equipping you with the tools to finally succeed.

Let's start by exploring the **7 reasons traditional diets have failed you**:

1. **They're one-size-fits-all**: These diets don't account for how endomorph body types, like yours, respond differently to food and exercise.

2. **They slow your metabolism**: Overly restrictive diets often trigger your body's survival mode, causing it to store fat instead of burn it.

3. **They don't consider hormonal shifts**: After 50, hormones like estrogen, cortisol, and insulin significantly influence weight and energy.

4. **They focus on deprivation, not nourishment**: Cutting entire food groups often leads to cravings and frustration.

5. **They ignore real-life challenges**: Stress, busy schedules, and emotional eating are rarely addressed in quick-fix plans.

6. **They lack sustainability**: The moment you stop following their rigid rules, the weight returns.

7. **They work against your body**: Instead of supporting your metabolism, they create long-term damage.

Now, here's what no one told you: Your metabolism isn't broken. It's adaptable. This means that with the right strategies—ones you'll learn throughout this book—you can reset it and start working *with* your body instead of against it.

That's where the **A.D.A.P.T.I.V.E. Metabolic System** comes in. Unlike anything you've tried before, this approach isn't a rigid set of rules. Instead, it's a flexible, personalized framework built around the pillars of **Active Metabolic Fluctuation, Dietary Freedom, Age-Specific Hormonal Balancing**, and more. You'll discover how these elements work together in upcoming chapters to help you fuel your body, balance your hormones, and transform your health.

For now, know this: the challenges you've faced aren't your fault. They're the result of outdated advice that didn't consider the unique metabolic and hormonal needs of women over 50. The strategies in this book will not only address those needs but also empower you to create sustainable change.

As we move forward, I'll show you how to apply these principles in practical, enjoyable ways. From understanding your metabolism (Chapter 3) to using meal planning tools (Chapter 9) and discovering recipes you'll love (Chapter 15), every step is designed to fit seamlessly into your life.

This isn't just another diet. It's a roadmap to lasting energy, confidence, and health. And it all starts now. Let's rewrite your story together.

2. You're Not Broken: Why Your Body Type Is a Gift in Disguise

It's time to change the narrative about your body. For too long, endomorphs have been told they're at a disadvantage—"your metabolism is slow," "your body clings to fat," "you can't lose weight easily." These statements aren't just disheartening—they're misleading. The truth is, your body isn't broken; it's uniquely equipped with strengths that, when properly understood, can lead to incredible results. Let's bust some myths and uncover the hidden potential of your endomorph body.

The 3 Lies You've Been Told About Your Endomorph Body

1. **"You'll always struggle with weight."** This is the most damaging lie of all. While endomorphs may store fat more easily, this isn't a life sentence. With the right approach, your metabolism can be activated to burn fat efficiently.

2. **"You're stuck with a slow metabolism."** Your metabolism isn't fixed; it's adaptable. Using strategies like metabolic fluctuation (explored in Chapter 6), you can train your body to speed up fat burning.

3. **"Your body works against you."** In reality, your body's ability to store energy is a survival advantage. With the right tools, this "stubborn fat" can become a steady fuel source for energy and fat loss.

Turning "Slow Metabolism" Into Your Biggest Strength

Your so-called slow metabolism is actually a built-in efficiency system. While traditional diets push your body into overdrive (and eventual burnout), the *A.D.A.P.T.I.V.E. Metabolic System* teaches you to work with this efficiency. By cycling macronutrients and embracing dietary freedom, you'll fuel your body in ways that optimize energy and fat burning—without deprivation or exhaustion.

How to Turn Your "Stubborn Fat" Into Your Secret Weapon

Stubborn fat is your body's way of preserving energy for tough times. The key to unlocking it? **Balance**. By focusing on hormonal support (like we'll cover in Chapter 8), stress management (Chapter 10), and consistent, sustainable changes, you'll train your body to use this stored fat as a powerful energy source. It's not about fighting your body—it's about guiding it.

In the chapters ahead, you'll learn how to harness these strengths to your advantage. Your endomorph body isn't a limitation—it's a foundation for long-term health and vitality. Let's transform the way you see yourself, **one step at a time**.

Part One

Understanding Your Over-50 Body

3. What Happens to Your Metabolism After 50 (And How to Take Back Control)

As you enter your 50s, you may notice that weight gain feels almost inevitable, even if your eating habits haven't changed. That's because your metabolism undergoes significant shifts during this time. But here's the empowering truth: these changes aren't permanent roadblocks—they're signals that your body needs a different approach. Understanding what's happening is the first step to regaining control.

The 5 Hormones Keeping You Stuck

Your metabolism is heavily influenced by hormones, and after 50, five key players can either help or hinder your progress:

1. **Estrogen**: As levels drop during menopause, your body tends to store more fat around the abdomen.

2. **Progesterone**: Its decline can lead to water retention and bloating, making you feel heavier.

3. **Cortisol**: Chronic stress raises this hormone, which encourages fat storage and muscle breakdown.

4. **Insulin**: Hormonal changes can make your cells more resistant to insulin, leading to fat gain and energy crashes.

5. **Thyroid Hormones**: A slower thyroid reduces your metabolic rate, making weight loss more challenging.

The good news is that with the right strategies you can manage these hormones effectively, helping your metabolism work *with* you.

The Most Overlooked Causes of Post-Menopausal Weight Gain

Hormonal shifts aren't the only factor at play. Other hidden causes often go unnoticed:

- **Muscle Loss**: After 50, muscle mass naturally declines, which slows your resting metabolic rate. Incorporating strength-building exercises (Chapter 17) can reverse this trend.

- **Poor Sleep**: Changes in sleep patterns impact your metabolism and hunger hormones, leading to increased cravings and fatigue. A targeted sleep reset plan (Chapter 18) will help.

- **Chronic Stress**: Emotional and physical stress not only raise cortisol but also encourage emotional eating, creating a cycle that feels impossible to break.
  Addressing these overlooked areas is crucial for taking back control of your body.

Why Your Metabolism Feels "Broken" (and How to Reset It in Weeks)

You might feel like your metabolism has slowed to a crawl, but it's not broken—it's adaptable. The real issue lies in years of traditional diets and lifestyle habits that may have trained your body to conserve energy rather than burn it. Resetting your metabolism involves creating a supportive environment for it to thrive.

- **Start With Food**: By embracing the principles of Active Metabolic Fluctuation (Chapter 6), you'll train your body to burn fat efficiently without feeling deprived.

- **Balance Hormones Naturally**: Eating nutrient-dense foods that stabilize insulin and cortisol (Chapter 8) will create a foundation for metabolic health.

- **Build Strength and Movement**: Muscle is your metabolism's best friend. Even short, simple strength-building routines can reignite your body's fat-burning potential.

These changes don't have to be overwhelming. Small, consistent adjustments can deliver noticeable results in just a few weeks. As you progress through this book, you'll uncover a step-by-step plan tailored specifically for your body and lifestyle.

Your metabolism isn't a lost cause—it's a work in progress. By understanding its needs and responding with targeted solutions, you'll rediscover your body's incredible capacity for energy, vitality, and transformation.

4. The Silent Saboteurs You Need to Stop Ignoring

Even if you're eating well and staying active, invisible barriers can silently sabotage your progress. Stress, poor sleep, and emotional eating aren't just inconvenient—they actively disrupt your body's ability to lose weight and maintain energy. Once you understand their impact and how to counteract them, you'll regain control over your health journey.

The 3 Ways Stress Wrecks Your Progress (and How to Fight Back)

Stress doesn't just feel overwhelming—it disrupts nearly every aspect of your metabolism. When your body senses stress, it releases cortisol to prepare for a "fight or flight" response. While this can be helpful in short bursts, chronic stress creates lasting issues:

1. **Fat Storage**: High cortisol encourages your body to store fat, especially around the abdomen.

2. **Muscle Loss**: When stress diverts energy, your muscles don't get the support they need for repair and growth.

3. **Cravings**: Cortisol spikes often trigger intense hunger for high-sugar or high-fat foods as your body seeks quick energy.

Reducing stress doesn't require major lifestyle changes. Simple practices like deep breathing, taking breaks, or even enjoying a moment of mindfulness can have a powerful impact. The key is consistency—small steps done daily can make all the difference.

Poor Sleep: The Invisible Weight-Loss Killer

If you're not getting enough quality sleep, your body's signals for hunger and energy become imbalanced. Sleep deprivation disrupts hormones like leptin, which signals fullness, and ghrelin, which increases hunger. Here's what happens when sleep is neglected:

- Increased Appetite: You're more likely to feel hungry and crave unhealthy snacks.

- Energy Dips: Fatigue makes it harder to stay active or motivated.

- Fat Storage: Insulin resistance caused by poor sleep leads to more fat being stored rather than burned.

Restoring good sleep habits is a game-changer. Create a nighttime routine that helps you wind down, whether that's reading, meditating, or avoiding screens. Over time, better sleep doesn't just improve your mood—it also gives your metabolism the reset it needs to function optimally.

Emotional Eating and Its Secret Triggers—And How to Break Free

We all turn to food for comfort occasionally, but when it becomes a habit, it can lead to frustration and guilt. Emotional eating is often driven by triggers you may not even notice:

1. **Stress and Anxiety**: When life feels overwhelming, food provides a temporary boost of dopamine—a natural "feel-good" chemical.

2. **Habits and Routines**: Associating certain activities, like watching TV, with snacking can create a cycle that's hard to break.

3. **Hidden Emotions**: Feelings of loneliness, boredom, or even unacknowledged stress can fuel unconscious eating habits.

Breaking free starts with identifying the triggers. Keep a log of your emotional eating patterns, and when you notice the urge to snack, pause and ask yourself: *Am I truly hungry, or is this emotional?* Replace the habit with an activity that nourishes your mind instead of just your stomach—like calling a friend or stepping outside for fresh air.

Part Two

The A.D.A.P.T.I.V.E. Metabolic System

5. The A.D.A.P.T.I.V.E. System Explained

When it comes to lasting health and weight loss, one-size-fits-all solutions just don't work—especially for women over 50. Your body has unique needs that change with age, hormones, and lifestyle. That's why the *A.D.A.P.T.I.V.E. Metabolic System* is different. It's designed to be flexible, empowering you to work with your body's natural rhythms to reset and recharge your metabolism.

The 8 Core Pillars to Reset and Recharge Your Metabolism

Each letter in *A.D.A.P.T.I.V.E.* represents a foundational pillar that supports your health and weight-loss goals:

1. **Active Metabolic Fluctuation**: By varying your macronutrient intake and activity levels, you keep your metabolism guessing, preventing it from stalling.

2. **Dietary Freedom Through Structure**: Instead of restrictive rules, this approach emphasizes balanced meals that nourish your body and fit your lifestyle.

3. **Age-Specific Hormonal Balancing**: Focused on the unique hormonal challenges women over 50 face, this pillar incorporates foods and habits to support hormonal health.

4. **Personalized Meal Planning**: No cookie-cutter diets here—you'll learn to create meals that align with your goals and preferences.

5. **Tactical Stress Management**: Reducing stress isn't optional—it's essential for maintaining hormonal balance and metabolic health.

6. **Incremental Lifestyle Tweaks**: Small, manageable changes add up to sustainable long-term success.

7. **Vitality Over Weight Loss**: Shifting your focus from the scale to energy, confidence, and quality of life creates more meaningful, lasting motivation.

8. **Empower Your Transformation**: Practical strategies, tools, and support ensure you're equipped to succeed no matter what challenges arise.

These pillars aren't just concepts—they're actionable steps that will guide you through the rest of this book, helping you take control of your health in a way that feels sustainable and empowering.

Why Adaptability Is the Secret to Success

Adaptability is the heart of the *A.D.A.P.T.I.V.E.* System. Think of it as a flexible framework rather than a rigid set of rules. Why is this so important? Because your body is constantly changing. Factors like stress, sleep, hormones, and activity levels can vary from day to day, and the most successful plans are those that adjust with you.

Traditional diets fail because they demand perfection. They expect you to eat the same way every day, exercise the same amount, and ignore how you're feeling. But life doesn't work that way, and neither does your metabolism.

The *A.D.A.P.T.I.V.E.* System encourages you to listen to your body and respond to its needs. For example, on high-stress days, your focus might shift to calming activities and nourishing meals that stabilize cortisol. On days when you feel energized, you can incorporate more intense activity or experiment with macronutrient cycling to optimize fat burning.

This flexibility doesn't just make the system easier to follow—it makes it more effective. By working with your body's natural rhythms, you create an environment where your metabolism thrives.

How to Work With Your Body, Not Against It

The most important shift you'll make is learning to stop fighting your body and start supporting it. Too often, diets treat your body like the enemy, forcing it into submission with extreme calorie cuts or excessive exercise. This creates a battle where no one wins.

With the *A.D.A.P.T.I.V.E.* System, the focus shifts to understanding your body's unique needs and giving it what it requires to function at its best. Here's how:

- **Respect Your Hormones**: Hormonal health is the foundation of metabolic health. When you eat in a way that balances insulin, cortisol, and estrogen, your body becomes more efficient at burning fat and maintaining energy.

- **Embrace Nourishment Over Restriction**: Instead of depriving your body, fuel it with nutrient-dense foods that satisfy your cravings and provide lasting energy.

- **Focus on Progress, Not Perfection**: Small, consistent changes build momentum. You don't have to be perfect to see results—every positive choice moves you closer to your goals.

This shift in mindset isn't just transformative for your metabolism—it's freeing. When you stop seeing your body as a problem to fix and start viewing it as a partner in your health journey, everything changes.

Your Next Steps

As you dive deeper into the *A.D.A.P.T.I.V.E.* System in the upcoming chapters, you'll learn how to put each of these pillars into practice. From balancing hormones and meal planning to reducing stress and building strength, every step is designed to support your body's natural abilities.

This is more than just a guide—it's a partnership between you and your body. Together, you'll unlock the energy, vitality, and confidence that have been waiting all along. The journey starts now!

6. A: Active Metabolic Fluctuation

One of the most powerful ways to reset and recharge your metabolism is by keeping it guessing. That's the foundation of Active Metabolic Fluctuation (AMF). Unlike traditional approaches that demand rigid eating patterns, AMF helps you balance consistency with variation, so your body never becomes too comfortable or resistant to fat loss. This flexibility doesn't just prevent plateaus—it makes the process more enjoyable and sustainable.

The 3-Phase Plan to Keep Your Body Guessing and Burning Fat

Active Metabolic Fluctuation is built around a three-phase plan designed to optimize fat burning:

1. **Preparation Phase**: In this phase, you focus on nourishing your body and building metabolic resilience. By prioritizing nutrient-dense foods, you'll stabilize blood sugar, balance hormones, and create a foundation for success.

2. **Acceleration Phase**: Here, you introduce targeted fluctuations in your macronutrient intake (proteins, carbs, and fats). This keeps your metabolism active, encouraging your body to burn fat more efficiently.

3. **Recovery Phase**: Recovery is just as important as acceleration. In this phase, you allow your body to rest and repair, ensuring you avoid burnout and maintain long-term energy.

How to Rotate Macronutrients Without Feeling Deprived

Rotating macronutrients is a key component of AMF. While it might sound complicated, it's a simple, practical strategy that aligns with your body's needs. Instead of cutting out entire food groups, you'll alternate your focus between higher-carb and lower-carb days. This variation helps your body burn fat while preserving muscle and keeping your energy levels stable.

Here's how it works:

- **Higher-Carb Days**: These days provide your body with the energy it needs for intense activities or strength training. Carbs fuel your muscles and replenish glycogen stores, leaving you feeling strong and energized.

- **Lower-Carb Days**: On these days, your body relies more on fat for energy, which accelerates fat loss. You'll still include healthy carbs, but the focus shifts to proteins and fats.

The beauty of this approach is its flexibility. You don't have to follow a rigid schedule—instead, you can adjust based on your activity levels, energy, and preferences. By doing so, you avoid the feelings of deprivation that come with restrictive diets, making it easier to stay consistent.

The Secret to Supercharging Fat Loss While Sleeping

Your metabolism doesn't stop when you go to bed—in fact, your body continues to burn calories and repair itself during sleep. The secret to maximizing fat loss during this time lies in creating the right conditions before bedtime.

1. **Evening Protein Intake**: Eating a protein-rich meal or snack before bed helps your body repair muscles and maintain metabolic activity throughout the night.

2. **Cortisol Management**: Lowering stress levels in the evening reduces cortisol, allowing your body to focus on fat burning instead of fat storage. Try calming activities like meditation, journaling, or light stretching to unwind.

3. **Consistent Sleep Routine**: Prioritizing quality sleep boosts hormones like growth hormone, which supports fat loss and muscle repair.

7. D: Dietary Freedom Through Structure

Dietary freedom doesn't mean chaos—it means simplicity and flexibility within a clear framework. With the right structure, eating becomes a source of nourishment, not stress. This is the foundation of *Dietary Freedom Through Structure*: a straightforward approach that lets you enjoy food while making choices that support your health and goals.

The 4 Food Rules That Make Eating Simple

You don't need complicated formulas or restrictive meal plans to eat well. These four food rules create a simple guide you can rely on every day:

1. **Prioritize Protein**: Protein is the cornerstone of every meal. It helps repair muscles, keeps you full longer, and stabilizes your blood sugar. Think of options like eggs, chicken, fish, tofu, or lentils as your foundation.

2. **Embrace Healthy Fats**: Don't shy away from fats—they're essential for brain health, hormone production, and satiety. Include sources like avocados, nuts, seeds, and olive oil.

3. **Fill Half Your Plate with Vegetables**: Vegetables provide fiber, vitamins, and minerals, making them essential for digestion and overall health. Aim for a colorful variety to maximize nutrients.

4. **Enjoy Smart Carbs**: Carbohydrates aren't your enemy. Whole grains, sweet potatoes, and fruits are nutrient-rich sources of energy that fuel your body effectively.

These rules are easy to remember and versatile, giving you the freedom to create meals that work for your tastes, schedule, and lifestyle.

How to Build Balanced Meals in Under 10 Minutes

Eating healthy doesn't have to be time-consuming. With a little preparation and the right ingredients, you can whip up a balanced meal in no time. Here's a quick formula to follow:

1. **Start with Protein**: Cooked chicken, a can of tuna, or scrambled eggs can be ready in minutes.

2. **Add Healthy Fats**: Drizzle olive oil on your salad, sprinkle seeds over your veggies, or slice up half an avocado.

3. **Include Veggies**: Pre-washed greens, steamed broccoli, or roasted peppers can save you time while adding flavor and nutrients.

4. **Top with Smart Carbs**: Add a small portion of quinoa, brown rice, or a piece of whole-grain toast to round out your meal.

Example: In less than 10 minutes, you could combine a handful of spinach, grilled salmon, a drizzle of olive oil, and roasted sweet potatoes for a quick, delicious dinner. The key is keeping your kitchen stocked with go-to staples that make healthy eating effortless.

Why You Can—and Should—Enjoy Carbs Without Guilt

Carbs often get a bad reputation, especially in the world of weight loss, but they're an essential part of a balanced diet. When chosen wisely, carbohydrates fuel your brain, muscles, and metabolism. The key is understanding which carbs to prioritize and how to incorporate them without guilt.

- **Choose Whole Foods**: Focus on complex carbs like whole grains, legumes, and starchy vegetables. These provide steady energy and are packed with fiber and nutrients.

- **Pair with Protein and Fats**: Combining carbs with protein or fats slows digestion, preventing blood sugar spikes and keeping you full longer.

- **Listen to Your Body**: Pay attention to how different carbs make you feel. For instance, oatmeal might give you sustained energy, while processed snacks may leave you sluggish.

When you embrace carbs as part of a structured diet, they become a tool to enhance your health and vitality—not a source of stress.

8. A: Age-Specific Hormonal Balancing

As women age, hormonal changes can feel like a roadblock to weight loss and energy. However, these changes are not insurmountable. By supporting your body with the right foods and habits, you can balance your hormones, regain vitality, and optimize your metabolism. This is the essence of *Age-Specific Hormonal Balancing*.

The 5 Superfoods for Post-Menopausal Women

Certain foods stand out as powerful allies for women navigating post-menopause. These superfoods provide the nutrients your body needs to thrive during this phase of life:

1. **Flaxseeds**: Rich in phytoestrogens, flaxseeds can help balance declining estrogen levels while providing fiber for improved digestion.

2. **Salmon**: Packed with omega-3 fatty acids, salmon supports heart health, reduces inflammation, and enhances brain function.

3. **Leafy Greens**: Spinach, kale, and Swiss chard are rich in calcium and magnesium, essential for bone health and muscle relaxation.

4. **Berries**: Loaded with antioxidants, berries protect against oxidative stress and support skin health and immunity.

5. **Avocados**: High in healthy fats and potassium, avocados help stabilize blood sugar and promote hormone production.

Foods That Boost Estrogen, Reduce Cortisol, and Stabilize Insulin

Balancing hormones after 50 involves targeting three key areas: estrogen, cortisol, and insulin. Each of these plays a critical role in your metabolism and overall well-being.

1. **Boost Estrogen**: Declining estrogen levels can lead to weight gain, fatigue, and mood swings. Foods like soy (tofu, edamame), flaxseeds, and chickpeas are natural sources of phytoestrogens that can support hormonal balance.

2. **Reduce Cortisol**: Chronic stress elevates cortisol, which can lead to fat storage and muscle loss. Incorporate magnesium-rich foods like almonds, dark chocolate, and bananas to calm your body and mind.

3. **Stabilize Insulin**: Insulin resistance becomes more common with age, making it harder to manage weight. Focus on low-glycemic foods like quinoa, sweet potatoes, and legumes to keep blood sugar levels steady.

Daily Rituals to Keep Hormones in Check

Hormonal health isn't just about what you eat—it's also about how you live. Simple daily rituals can have a profound impact on your hormone balance:

1. **Start Your Day with Protein**: Eating a protein-rich breakfast sets the tone for stable blood sugar and energy throughout the day. Consider options like eggs, Greek yogurt, or a smoothie with protein powder.

2. **Practice Stress Management**: Even a few minutes of deep breathing, meditation, or journaling can lower cortisol levels and improve your mood.

3. **Move Your Body**: Gentle movement like yoga or walking can help regulate insulin and cortisol while boosting endorphins.

4. **Hydrate Mindfully**: Drinking water with a splash of lemon supports hydration and digestion, aiding overall metabolic health.

5. **Prioritize Sleep**: A consistent bedtime routine promotes restorative sleep, which is essential for hormonal regulation.

These small, manageable habits can create a ripple effect, improving not only your hormones but your overall quality of life.

9. P: Personalized Meal Planning Made Easy

Healthy eating doesn't have to feel overwhelming or rigid. *Personalized Meal Planning* is about creating a framework that fits your goals, lifestyle, and preferences while leaving room for flexibility. With just a few simple strategies, you can take the guesswork out of what to eat and start enjoying meals that fuel your body and bring you closer to your health goals.

The 3-Step Method to Design Meals for Your Goals

Creating balanced, goal-oriented meals is simpler than you think. This three-step method provides structure while giving you the freedom to make choices that suit your tastes:

1. **Choose a Protein Base**: Protein is the cornerstone of your meals. It supports muscle maintenance, keeps you full longer, and stabilizes blood sugar. Select lean options like chicken, fish, eggs, or plant-based proteins like tofu or lentils.

2. **Add Fiber and Color**: Vegetables and whole grains provide essential nutrients and keep your digestion on track. Aim to fill half your plate with colorful veggies, such as leafy greens, carrots, or peppers, and add a portion of fiber-rich grains like quinoa or brown rice.

3. **Include Healthy Fats**: Don't forget about fats—they're critical for hormone production and overall energy. A handful of nuts, a drizzle of olive oil, or some avocado slices can round out your meal beautifully.

This method isn't restrictive. Instead, it empowers you to build meals that are both nutritious and satisfying, no matter your dietary preferences.

Meal Timing for Maximum Energy and Recovery

When you eat is just as important as what you eat. Proper meal timing helps regulate blood sugar, maintain energy levels, and support recovery after physical activity. Here's how to time your meals effectively:

- **Start with a Protein-Rich Breakfast**: Eating protein in the morning jumpstarts your metabolism and keeps hunger at bay. A smoothie with Greek yogurt or scrambled eggs with spinach are excellent options.

- **Refuel Midday**: A balanced lunch that includes complex carbs, protein, and veggies provides sustained energy for the afternoon. Think grilled chicken with roasted sweet potatoes and steamed broccoli.

- **Focus on Recovery in the Evening**: A lighter dinner rich in protein and healthy fats aids muscle repair and prepares your body for restful sleep. Salmon with asparagus or a chickpea salad with olive oil are perfect choices.

Adapting Your Plan to Real-Life Challenges

Life doesn't always follow a perfect schedule, and neither will your meals. Flexibility is key to making personalized meal planning sustainable. Here are practical ways to adapt when challenges arise:

- **Busy Days**: Prepare quick options in advance, like pre-portioned salads, roasted veggies, or cooked quinoa. These can be assembled into a meal in minutes.

- **Dining Out**: When eating at restaurants, focus on protein-rich dishes and ask for extra vegetables instead of fries or bread. Don't stress about perfection—enjoy the experience and aim for balance.

- **Unexpected Changes**: If a meal doesn't go as planned, remember that one misstep won't derail your progress. Focus on making your next meal nourishing and aligned with your goals.

The goal is to build habits that support your health even when life gets hectic, ensuring you're always moving forward.

10. T: Tactical Stress Management

Stress is an unavoidable part of life, but it doesn't have to derail your progress. Tactical Stress Management is about equipping yourself with simple, effective tools to keep stress in check, support your hormones, and protect your metabolism. By learning to manage stress strategically, you'll not only feel better but also create an environment where your body can thrive.

Quick Techniques to Lower Cortisol in 10 Minutes

When stress strikes, cortisol—the stress hormone—spikes. High cortisol levels can lead to fat storage, cravings, and energy crashes. The good news? You can reduce cortisol in as little as 10 minutes with these quick techniques:

1. **Deep Breathing**: Take slow, deep breaths for a few minutes. Focus on inhaling for a count of four, holding for four, and exhaling for six. This calms your nervous system and lowers cortisol levels almost immediately.

2. **Mini Mindfulness Breaks**: Pause whatever you're doing and spend 10 minutes fully immersed in the present moment. Use an app like Calm or Headspace, or simply close your eyes and focus on your senses.

3. **Gratitude Journaling**: Write down three things you're grateful for. This shifts your focus away from stressors and boosts positive emotions, which naturally reduce cortisol.

Evening Rituals to Reset Your Metabolism

Evenings are a powerful opportunity to reset both your mind and metabolism. Creating a calming nightly routine helps lower cortisol, which in turn supports fat-burning and restorative sleep. Here are some ideas:

- **Unplug Early**: Turn off screens at least an hour before bed. Blue light disrupts your body's production of melatonin, the sleep hormone.

- **Soothing Activities**: Engage in relaxing activities like reading, light yoga, or taking a warm bath. These signal your body that it's time to wind down.

- **Bedtime Herbal Tea**: Sip on chamomile or lavender tea, which are known for their calming properties.

The Link Between Breathing and Fat Loss

Your breath is one of the most overlooked tools for supporting fat loss. Stress often leads to shallow, rapid breathing, which keeps your body in a heightened state of alertness. Deep, diaphragmatic breathing does the opposite—it relaxes your nervous system, lowers cortisol, and improves oxygen delivery to your cells, boosting fat-burning efficiency.

Try this simple exercise: Sit or lie comfortably, place a hand on your abdomen, and inhale deeply through your nose, letting your belly rise. Exhale slowly through your mouth, allowing your belly to fall. Repeat for 5–10 minutes daily to harness the fat-loss benefits of better breathing.

11. I: Incremental Lifestyle Tweaks

Transforming your health doesn't require an all-or-nothing approach. In fact, the most sustainable progress comes from small, intentional changes—what we call *Incremental Lifestyle Tweaks*. By building micro-habits that fit seamlessly into your routine, you create a foundation for long-term success without feeling overwhelmed or deprived.

The 3 Micro-Habits That Create Long-Term Success

1. **Start Your Day with Water**: Drinking a glass of water first thing in the morning kickstarts hydration, boosts energy, and supports metabolism. Add a squeeze of lemon for extra benefits.

2. **Take 5-Minute Movement Breaks**: Every hour, stand up, stretch, or take a short walk. These small bursts of movement improve circulation and prevent stiffness while boosting your mood.

3. **End the Day with Gratitude**: Before bed, jot down three things you're grateful for. This simple habit lowers stress and promotes a positive mindset, which impacts your overall health.

How to Add Movement, Mindfulness, and Joy to Your Day

Living a healthy life isn't just about what you eat—it's also about how you feel and move through your day. Here's how to integrate movement, mindfulness, and joy into your routine:

- **Movement**: Find activities you enjoy, like dancing, yoga, or walking your dog. The goal is to make movement something you look forward to, not a chore.

- **Mindfulness**: Set aside a few minutes each day to breathe deeply, meditate, or simply pause and reflect. This helps reduce stress and improves focus.

- **Joy**: Schedule time for things that bring you happiness, whether it's listening to music, gardening, or connecting with loved ones. Joy is as important as nutrition for your overall well-being.

Why Small Changes Lead to Big Wins

The power of incremental tweaks lies in their sustainability. Small changes are easy to implement and maintain, making them far more effective than drastic overhauls. For example, adding an extra serving of vegetables each day is more manageable—and impactful—than completely revamping your diet overnight.

Over time, these small steps build momentum. Each success reinforces the next, creating a ripple effect that transforms your health and well-being in ways you never thought possible.

Start small, stay consistent, and celebrate every win. The path to lasting health is made up of these little moments, and they're all within your reach.

12. V: Vitality Over Weight Loss

Focusing solely on the scale can be discouraging, especially when progress doesn't show up as a specific number. *Vitality Over Weight Loss* shifts your perspective from pounds to the things that truly matter—energy, confidence, and quality of life. By redefining success, you'll create a more positive and fulfilling relationship with your health journey.

The 4 Non-Scale Wins That Matter Most

1. **Increased Energy**: Notice how your energy levels improve as you fuel your body with balanced meals and better sleep. Waking up refreshed and staying active throughout the day is a huge success.

2. **Improved Mood**: Feeling calmer, happier, and less stressed are signs that your hormonal health is improving. These changes often happen before you see results on the scale.

3. **Better Mobility and Strength**: Moving more easily, feeling stronger, or being able to complete activities that once felt difficult are all meaningful indicators of progress.

4. **Health Markers**: Positive changes in blood pressure, cholesterol, or blood sugar levels are tangible signs that your body is thriving.

Why Energy, Confidence, and Quality of Life Are Your True Goals

The ultimate goal of any health journey should be to feel good in your body and enjoy life more fully.

- **Energy**: Imagine having the stamina to keep up with your family, tackle new adventures, or simply get through the day without feeling drained. That's vitality in action.

- **Confidence**: Feeling strong, capable, and comfortable in your skin is invaluable. Confidence radiates in everything you do.

- **Quality of Life**: Whether it's walking without pain, playing with your grandchildren, or traveling, focusing on life's joys makes every effort worth it.

These outcomes aren't measured by a scale—they're felt in your everyday life.

How to Measure Progress Without Obsessing Over the Scale

Ditching the scale doesn't mean ignoring progress. Instead, use methods that highlight your growth and keep you motivated:

- **Track Strength Gains**: Notice how your workouts improve, whether it's lifting heavier weights or walking longer distances.

- **Take Note of How You Feel**: Keep a journal to document your energy levels, mood, and sleep patterns over time.

- **Celebrate Milestones**: Recognize achievements like cooking healthier meals, sticking to a bedtime routine, or managing stress effectively.

13. E: Empower Your Transformation

Every journey comes with its challenges, but having the right tools can make all the difference. *Your Transformation Toolkit* is designed to help you navigate obstacles, stay on track, and keep building momentum. This section provides practical solutions for common pitfalls, empowering you to turn setbacks into comebacks.

5 Common Pitfalls and How to Overcome Them

1. **Hitting a Plateau**: Progress may slow at times, but plateaus are normal. Revisit your meal timing, add variety to your workouts, or adjust your macronutrient balance to reignite fat loss.

2. **Feeling Overwhelmed**: Tackling everything at once can feel daunting. Focus on one pillar at a time—like meal planning or stress management—before moving on to the next.

3. **Emotional Eating**: Stress or boredom can lead to unhealthy choices. Replace emotional eating with mindful alternatives, like journaling or a quick walk, to address the underlying feelings.

4. **Busy Schedules**: Life can get hectic, but prepping meals ahead or choosing quick, nutrient-dense options ensures you stay consistent.

5. **Losing Motivation**: Progress isn't always linear. Celebrate small wins and remind yourself why you started to reignite your drive.

A Personalized Metabolic Problem Solver for Every Challenge

Your body is unique, and so are the challenges you'll face. This toolkit equips you with personalized strategies to overcome them:

- **Low Energy**: If you're feeling drained, evaluate your sleep quality and ensure you're eating enough complex carbs for sustained energy.

- **Persistent Cravings**: Combat cravings with protein-rich snacks and healthy fats, which keep you fuller longer. Hydration is key too—sometimes thirst is mistaken for hunger.

- **Stress Management Struggles**: Incorporate daily mindfulness practices, like deep breathing or meditation, to reduce cortisol levels and improve focus.

- **Stalled Weight Loss**: Adjust your Active Metabolic Fluctuation plan to include more variation in macronutrient cycling or increase strength training to build muscle.

- **Lack of Time for Exercise**: Break your activity into smaller increments, like 10-minute sessions throughout the day. Movement doesn't have to be all at once to be effective.

How to Build Momentum and Stay Motivated

Momentum is built through small, consistent actions. Here's how to maintain it:

1. **Set Short-Term Goals**: Break your journey into smaller milestones. Instead of focusing solely on long-term outcomes, celebrate daily or weekly achievements.

2. **Track Your Progress**: Use a journal or app to log meals, energy levels, workouts, and mood. Seeing tangible improvements keeps you motivated.

3. **Find Accountability**: Share your goals with a friend or join a supportive community. Having someone cheer you on or share tips can make a big difference.

4. **Reward Yourself**: Recognize your hard work with non-food rewards, like a new workout outfit, a relaxing massage, or a fun activity you've been looking forward to.

Part Three

Eating to Fuel Your Transformation

14. The Endomorph's Guide to Food Freedom

Dieting as an endomorph can feel like navigating a minefield of misinformation. Traditional advice often ignores the unique needs of your body type, leading to frustration and setbacks. But *Food Freedom* isn't about deprivation—it's about learning what truly works for your metabolism and embracing a balanced, enjoyable way of eating.

The 5 Biggest Mistakes Endomorph Women Make When Dieting

1. **Overly Restrictive Diets**: Cutting out entire food groups or eating too few calories slows your metabolism and increases cravings. Instead, focus on balance and nourishment.

2. **Skipping Meals**: Skipping meals to "save calories" often leads to overeating later in the day. Consistent meals stabilize blood sugar and prevent energy crashes.

3. **Fearing Carbs**: Carbohydrates are often unfairly blamed for weight gain, but when chosen wisely, they provide essential energy and support hormonal health.

4. **Underestimating Protein Needs**: Many endomorph women don't consume enough protein, which is critical for building muscle, maintaining energy, and keeping you full.

5. **Relying on Fad Diets**: Quick-fix diets often create more harm than good, disrupting your metabolism and making long-term progress harder to achieve.

The Unknown Food Groups You Should Always Prioritize

To fuel your body and optimize your metabolism, prioritize these often-overlooked but essential food groups:

1. **Fiber-Rich Foods**: High-fiber vegetables, legumes, and whole grains support digestion, stabilize blood sugar, and keep you full. Examples include lentils, quinoa, and leafy greens.

2. **Healthy Fats**: Avocados, nuts, seeds, and olive oil provide energy and help regulate hormones like cortisol and insulin.

3. **Phytoestrogen Foods**: Foods like flaxseeds, tofu, and chickpeas naturally support estrogen levels, which can help balance hormones during menopause.

4. **Fermented Foods**: Yogurt, kimchi, and sauerkraut promote gut health, which is essential for efficient metabolism and overall well-being.

5. **Hydration-Boosting Fruits and Veggies**: Water-rich options like cucumbers, watermelon, and oranges keep you hydrated and energized throughout the day.

How to Tame Cravings Without Cutting Out Comfort Foods

Cravings are a natural part of life and shouldn't be a source of guilt. Instead of trying to eliminate them completely, learn how to manage them in a way that aligns with your goals:

1. **Balance Your Meals**: Cravings often stem from nutrient imbalances. Make sure each meal includes protein, healthy fats, and fiber to keep hunger and energy levels steady.

2. **Satisfy the Craving Smartly**: If you're craving something sweet, try a piece of dark chocolate or a yogurt parfait with berries. For salty snacks, air-popped popcorn or roasted chickpeas can hit the spot.

3. **Use the 80/20 Rule**: Aim to eat nourishing foods 80% of the time while allowing room for indulgences. Enjoy a slice of pizza or a dessert guilt-free—it's all about balance.

4. **Identify Emotional Triggers**: Sometimes cravings aren't about food at all. Pause and ask yourself if you're truly hungry or if stress or boredom might be the culprit.

5. **Stay Hydrated**: Dehydration can often masquerade as hunger. Start with a glass of water before reaching for a snack.

A New Way to Think About Food

Food freedom isn't about rigid rules or deprivation—it's about understanding your body and fueling it in a way that feels good and sustainable. By avoiding common dieting mistakes, prioritizing the right food groups, and learning to manage cravings, you can create a relationship with food that supports your goals while bringing joy to your meals.

In the chapters ahead, you'll explore recipes and meal planning strategies that make these principles easy to apply. Together, we'll turn food from a source of stress into a powerful tool for transformation.

100 Recipes You'll Love (and Actually Use)

I understand how important it is to visualize the dishes you're preparing, especially when embracing a new way of eating. That's why I've created an exclusive digital gallery, accessible through the QR code below. Not only can you view the images, but you can also download or share them to inspire others on their transformation journey.

These digital images give you the flexibility to use them however you need—whether you're in the kitchen cooking or browsing for ideas while planning your weekly meals.

20 Breakfasts That Jumpstart Your Day (and Your Hormones).

1. Greek Yogurt and Berry Power Bowl

Nutritional Information (Per Serving):

Calories: 220

Protein: 15g

Fat: 5g

Carbohydrates: 28g

Fiber: 5g

Sugar: 15g

Serving Size: Makes 1 bowl.

Prep and Cook Time:

Prep Time: 5 minutes

Cook Time: 0 minutes

Total Time: 5 minutes

Ingredients:

- 1 cup plain Greek yogurt (2%)
- ½ cup fresh mixed berries (blueberries, raspberries, strawberries)
- 1 tbsp chia seeds
- 1 tbsp crushed almonds
- 1 tsp honey or maple syrup (optional)

Instructions:

1. Place Greek yogurt in a bowl.
2. Top with mixed berries, chia seeds, and almonds.
3. Drizzle with honey or maple syrup if desired.

2. Avocado and Egg Breakfast Toast

Nutritional Information (Per Serving)

Calories: 290

Protein: 13g

Fat: 20g

Carbohydrates: 18g

Fiber: 6g

Sugar: 1g

Serving Size:

Makes 1 toast.

Prep and Cook Time:

Prep Time: 5 minutes   Total Time: 10 minutes

Cook Time: 5 minutes

Ingredients:

- 1 slice whole-grain bread, toasted
- ½ avocado, mashed
- 1 large egg, poached or fried
- 1 pinch red pepper flakes (optional)
- Salt and pepper to taste

Instructions:

1. Spread mashed avocado on the toasted bread.
2. Top with the poached or fried egg.
3. Season with red pepper flakes, salt, and pepper.

---

3. Spinach and Mushroom Breakfast Wrap

Nutritional Information (Per Serving):

Calories: 250   Carbohydrates: 22g

Protein: 16g   Fiber: 4g

Fat: 10g   Sugar: 2g

Serving Size:

Makes 1 wrap.

Prep and Cook Time:

Prep Time: 5 minutes   Total Time: 15 minutes

Cook Time: 10 minutes

Ingredients:

- 1 whole-grain tortilla
- 2 large eggs, scrambled
- ½ cup baby spinach
- ¼ cup sliced mushrooms, sautéed
- 2 tbsp shredded cheddar cheese

Instructions:

- Warm the tortilla in a skillet for 1 minute.
- Add scrambled eggs, spinach, mushrooms, and cheese.
- Roll into a wrap and serve warm.

4. Sweet Potato and Kale Breakfast Hash

Nutritional Information (Per Serving):

Calories: 180Protein: 8g

Fiber: 4g

Carbohydrates: 25g

Sugar: 5g

Serving Size:

Makes 2 servings.

Prep and Cook Time:

Prep Time: 10 minutes

Total Time: 25 minutes

Cook Time: 15 minutes

Ingredients:

- 1 medium sweet potato, diced
- 1 cup chopped kale
- 2 large eggs
- 1 tbsp olive oil
- Salt and pepper to taste

Instructions:

1. Heat olive oil in a skillet and sauté sweet potato for 10 minutes.
2. Add kale and cook until wilted, about 5 minutes.
3. Serve with eggs cooked to your preference.

5. Banana and Almond Butter Smoothie

Nutritional Information (Per Serving):

Calories: 250

Protein: 12g

Fat: 10g

Carbohydrates: 30g

Fiber: 6g

Sugar: 14g

Serving Size:

Makes 1 smoothie.

Prep and Cook Time:

Prep Time: 5 minutes

Cook Time: 0 minutes

Total Time: 5 minutes

Ingredients:

- 1 medium banana
- 1 cup unsweetened almond milk
- 1 tbsp almond butter
- 1 scoop vanilla protein powder
- ½ tsp cinnamon

Instructions:

1. Combine all ingredients in a blender.
2. Blend until smooth and serve.

6. Quinoa Breakfast Bowl with Berries and Almonds

Nutritional Information (Per Serving):

Calories: 270

Protein: 10g

Fat: 8g

Carbohydrates: 40g

Fiber: 6g

Sugar: 10g

Serving Size:

Makes 1 bowl.

Emma Grace Stanton

Prep and Cook Time:

Prep Time: 5 minutes

Cook Time: 15 minutes

Total Time: 20 minutes

Ingredients:

- ½ cup cooked quinoa
- ½ cup mixed berries
- 1 tbsp sliced almonds

- 1 tsp honey
- ¼ cup almond milk

Instructions:

1. Place quinoa in a bowl.
2. Top with berries, almonds, and honey.
3. Pour almond milk over and serve.

---

7. Cottage Cheese and Pineapple Bowl

Nutritional Information (Per Serving):

Calories: 200

Protein: 15g

Fat: 5g

Carbohydrates: 22g

Fiber: 2g

Sugar: 15g

Serving Size:

Makes 1 bowl.

Prep and Cook Time:

Prep Time: 5 minutes

Cook Time: 0 minutes

Total Time: 5 minutes

Ingredients:

- ½ cup cottage cheese
- ½ cup fresh pineapple chunks

- 1 tbsp chia seeds
- 1 tsp shredded coconut

Instructions:

1. Combine cottage cheese and pineapple in a bowl.

2. Sprinkle with chia seeds and coconut. Serve chilled.

---

8. Oatmeal with Apple and Walnuts

Nutritional Information (Per Serving):

Calories: 240

Protein: 8g

Fat: 9g

Carbohydrates: 34g

Fiber: 5g

Sugar: 10g

Serving Size:

Makes 1 serving.

Prep and Cook Time:

Prep Time: 5 minutes

Cook Time: 5 minutes

Total Time: 10 minutes

Ingredients:

- ½ cup rolled oats

- 1 cup water or almond milk

- ½ apple, diced

- 1 tbsp chopped walnuts

- 1 tsp cinnamon

Instructions:

1. Cook oats in water or almond milk according to package instructions.

2. Top with apple, walnuts, and cinnamon.

---

9. Smoked Salmon and Avocado Breakfast Plate

Nutritional Information (Per Serving):

Calories: 280

Protein: 18g

Fat: 18g

Carbohydrates: 8g

Fiber: 4g

Sugar: 1g

Serving Size:

Makes 1 serving.

Prep and Cook Time:

Prep Time: 5 minutes

Total Time: 5 minutes

Cook Time: 0 minutes

Ingredients:

- 2 oz smoked salmon
- ½ avocado, sliced
- 1 cup arugula or mixed greens
- 1 tsp olive oil
- Lemon wedge

Instructions:

1. Arrange smoked salmon, avocado, and greens on a plate.

2. Drizzle with olive oil and squeeze lemon over the top.

---

10. Protein-Packed Chia Seed Pudding

Nutritional Information (Per Serving):

Calories: 210

Carbohydrates: 24g

Protein: 10g

Fiber: 8g

Fat: 10g

Sugar: 6g

Serving Size:

Makes 2 servings.

Prep and Cook Time:

Prep Time: 5 minutes

Total Time: Overnight

Cook Time: 0 minutes (overnight chilling)

Ingredients:

- ¼ cup chia seeds
- 1 cup unsweetened almond milk

- 1 tbsp maple syrup
- ½ tsp vanilla extract
- Fresh berries for topping

Instructions:

1. Combine chia seeds, almond milk, maple syrup, and vanilla in a jar.

2. Stir well, cover, and refrigerate overnight.

3. Top with fresh berries before serving.

---

11. Zucchini and Cheese Frittata

Nutritional Information (Per Serving):

Calories: 190

Protein: 14g

Fat: 12g

Carbohydrates: 6g

Fiber: 2g

Sugar: 2g

Serving Size:

Makes 4 servings.

Prep and Cook Time:

Prep Time: 10 minutes

Cook Time: 20 minutes

Total Time: 30 minutes

Ingredients:

- 6 large eggs
- 1 cup grated zucchini, squeezed to remove excess water
- ½ cup shredded mozzarella
- ¼ cup diced onion
- 1 tbsp olive oil
- ¼ tsp salt
- ¼ tsp black pepper

Instructions:

1. Preheat the oven to 375°F (190°C).

2. Heat olive oil in an oven-safe skillet and sauté onion until soft.

3. In a bowl, whisk eggs, zucchini, mozzarella, salt, and pepper. Pour into skillet.

4. Bake for 20 minutes or until set. Slice and serve.

---

12. Peanut Butter and Banana Protein Pancakes

Nutritional Information (Per Serving):

Calories: 240

Protein: 12g

Fat: 8g

Carbohydrates: 30g

Fiber: 5g

Sugar: 10g

Serving Size:

Makes 2 servings (4 small pancakes).

Prep and Cook Time:

Prep Time: 5 minutes

Cook Time: 10 minutes

Total Time: 15 minutes

Ingredients:

- 1 medium banana, mashed
- 1 large egg
- 2 tbsp peanut butter
- ½ cup rolled oats
- ½ tsp baking powder

Instructions:

1. Combine all ingredients in a blender until smooth.

2. Cook batter in a non-stick skillet over medium heat, flipping once bubbles form. Serve warm.

---

13. Savory Breakfast Quinoa Bowl

Nutritional Information (Per Serving):

Calories: 220

Protein: 12g

Fat: 7g

Carbohydrates: 28g

Fiber: 4g

Sugar: 2g

Serving Size:

Makes 1 bowl.

Prep and Cook Time:

Prep Time: 10 minutes

Cook Time: 15 minutes

Total Time: 25 minutes

Ingredients:

- ½ cup cooked quinoa
- 1 large egg, fried
- ¼ avocado, sliced
- 2 tbsp crumbled feta cheese
- 1 tbsp olive oil

Instructions:

3. Place cooked quinoa in a bowl.
4. Top with fried egg, avocado, feta, and drizzle with olive oil. Serve warm.

---

14. Apple Cinnamon Overnight Oats

Nutritional Information (Per Serving):

Calories: 200

Protein: 8g

Fat: 4g

Carbohydrates: 34g

Fiber: 6g

Sugar: 12g

Serving Size:

Makes 2 servings.

Prep and Cook Time:

Prep Time: 5 minutes

Cook Time: 0 minutes (overnight chilling)

Total Time: Overnight

Ingredients:

- ½ cup rolled oats
- ½ cup unsweetened almond milk

- ½ apple, diced
- 1 tsp cinnamon
- 1 tsp honey

Instructions:

4. Combine oats, almond milk, apple, cinnamon, and honey in a jar.

5. Stir, cover, and refrigerate overnight. Serve chilled or warmed.

---

15. Turkey and Veggie Breakfast Scramble

Nutritional Information (Per Serving):

Calories: 180

Carbohydrates: 5g

Protein: 20g

Fiber: 2g

Fat: 6g

Sugar: 1g

Serving Size:

Makes 1 serving.

Prep and Cook Time:

Prep Time: 5 minutes

Total Time: 15 minutes

Cook Time: 10 minutes

Ingredients:

- 2 large egg whites
- 2 oz ground turkey
- ½ cup chopped bell pepper
- ½ cup baby spinach
- 1 tsp olive oil

Instructions:

1. Heat olive oil in a skillet and cook turkey until browned.

2. Add bell pepper and spinach, cooking until softened.

3. Stir in egg whites and cook until set.

---

16. Pumpkin Spice Chia Pudding

Nutritional Information (Per Serving):

Calories: 220

Carbohydrates: 30g

Protein: 8g

Fiber: 8g

Fat: 9g

Sugar: 10g

Serving Size:

Makes 2 servings.

Prep and Cook Time:

Prep Time: 5 minutes

Total Time: Overnight

Cook Time: 0 minutes (overnight chilling)

Ingredients:

- ¼ cup chia seeds
- 1 cup unsweetened almond milk
- ¼ cup pumpkin puree
- ½ tsp pumpkin spice
- 1 tsp maple syrup

Instructions:

1. Mix chia seeds, almond milk, pumpkin puree, pumpkin spice, and maple syrup in a jar.

2. Refrigerate overnight. Serve with a sprinkle of cinnamon.

---

17. Blueberry Almond Breakfast Smoothie

Nutritional Information (Per Serving):

Calories: 210

Carbohydrates: 28g

Protein: 10g

Fiber: 5g

Fat: 8g

Sugar: 14g

Serving Size:

Makes 1 smoothie.

Prep and Cook Time:

Prep Time: 5 minutes

Total Time: 5 minutes

Cook Time: 0 minutes

Ingredients:

- ½ cup frozen blueberries
- 1 cup unsweetened almond milk
- 1 tbsp almond butter
- 1 tbsp chia seeds
- 1 scoop vanilla protein powder

Instructions:

1. Blend all ingredients until smooth. Serve immediately.

---

18. Mushroom and Goat Cheese Omelette

Nutritional Information (Per Serving):

Calories: 210

Carbohydrates: 3g

Protein: 14g

Fiber: 1g

Fat: 16g

Sugar: 1g

Serving Size:

Makes 1 omelette.

Prep and Cook Time:

Prep Time: 5 minutes

Total Time: 15 minutes

Cook Time: 10 minutes

Ingredients:

- 2 large eggs
- ¼ cup sliced mushrooms
- 1 tbsp crumbled goat cheese
- 1 tsp butter

Instructions:

1. Sauté mushrooms in butter until softened.
2. Whisk eggs and pour into the skillet.

3. Add goat cheese and cook until set.

---

19. Whole-Grain Waffles with Nut Butter

Nutritional Information (Per Serving):

Calories: 260

Protein: 10g

Fiber: 5g

Fat: 12g

Sugar: 5g

Carbohydrates: 28g

Serving Size:

Makes 2 waffles.

Prep and Cook Time:

Prep Time: 5 minutes

Total Time: 15 minutes

Cook Time: 10 minutes

Ingredients:

- ½ cup whole-grain waffle mix
- 1 tbsp almond butter
- ½ cup unsweetened almond milk
- 1 tbsp chopped nuts

Instructions:

1. Prepare waffles according to package instructions.

2. Top with almond butter and chopped nuts before serving.

---

20. Breakfast Stuffed Bell Peppers

Nutritional Information (Per Serving):

Calories: 190

Carbohydrates: 15g

Protein: 15g

Fiber: 4g

Fat: 8g

Sugar: 6g

Serving Size:

Makes 2 stuffed peppers.

Prep and Cook Time:

Prep Time: 10 minutes

Cook Time: 20 minutes

Total Time: 30 minutes

Ingredients:

- 2 bell peppers, halved and deseeded
- 3 large eggs
- 2 tbsp shredded cheddar cheese
- 1 cup baby spinach, chopped
- Salt and pepper to taste

Instructions:

1. Preheat oven to 375°F (190°C). Place bell pepper halves on a baking sheet.

2. Whisk eggs, spinach, cheese, salt, and pepper. Fill peppers with mixture.

3. Bake for 20 minutes or until eggs are set.

30 Easy Lunches for Busy Days

1. Grilled Chicken and Avocado Salad

Nutritional Information (Per Serving):

Calories: 310

Protein: 25g

Fat: 18g

Carbohydrates: 12g

Fiber: 6g

Sugar: 2g

Serving Size:

Makes 2 servings.

Prep and Cook Time:

Prep Time: 10 minutes

Cook Time: 10 minutes

Total Time: 20 minutes

Ingredients:

- 2 cups mixed greens
- 1 grilled chicken breast, sliced
- ½ avocado, diced
- ¼ cup cherry tomatoes, halved
- 1 tbsp olive oil
- 1 tsp balsamic vinegar

Instructions:

1. Arrange mixed greens on a plate.
2. Top with chicken, avocado, and cherry tomatoes.
3. Drizzle with olive oil and balsamic vinegar. Serve immediately.

---

2. Lentil and Spinach Soup

Nutritional Information (Per Serving):

Calories: 250

Protein: 14g

Fat: 6g

Carbohydrates: 35g

Fiber: 12g

Sugar: 4g

Serving Size:

Makes 4 servings.

Prep and Cook Time:

Prep Time: 10 minutes

Cook Time: 25 minutes

Total Time: 35 minutes

Ingredients:

- 1 cup dry lentils, rinsed
- 4 cups vegetable broth
- 2 cups fresh spinach
- 1 diced carrot
- 1 diced onion
- 1 tbsp olive oil
- 1 tsp cumin

Instructions:

1. Heat olive oil in a pot and sauté onion and carrot until soft.
2. Add lentils, broth, and cumin. Simmer for 20 minutes.
3. Stir in spinach and cook for 5 minutes. Serve warm.

---

3. Turkey and Hummus Wrap

Nutritional Information (Per Serving):

Calories: 280

Protein: 20g

Fat: 10g

Carbohydrates: 28g

Fiber: 5g

Sugar: 2g

Serving Size:

Makes 1 wrap.

Prep and Cook Time:

Prep Time: 5 minutes

Cook Time: 0 minutes

Total Time: 5 minutes

Ingredients:

- 1 whole-grain tortilla
- 2 oz sliced turkey
- 2 tbsp hummus
- ¼ cup shredded lettuce
- ¼ cup diced cucumber

Instructions:

1. Spread hummus on the tortilla.
2. Add turkey, lettuce, and cucumber. Roll into a wrap and serve.

---

4. Quinoa and Black Bean Salad

Nutritional Information (Per Serving):

Calories: 320

Protein: 12g

Fat: 10g

Carbohydrates: 45g

Fiber: 8g

Sugar: 4g

Serving Size:

Makes 2 servings.

Prep and Cook Time:

Prep Time: 10 minutes

Cook Time: 15 minutes

Total Time: 25 minutes

Ingredients:

- 1 cup cooked quinoa
- ½ cup black beans, rinsed
- ½ cup diced bell pepper
- 1 tbsp olive oil
- 1 tbsp lime juice
- 1 tsp cumin

Instructions:

1. Combine quinoa, black beans, and bell pepper in a bowl.

2. Drizzle with olive oil and lime juice. Toss with cumin and serve chilled.

---

5. Grilled Salmon with Asparagus

Nutritional Information (Per Serving):

Calories: 310

Carbohydrates: 8g

Protein: 25g

Fiber: 4g

Fat: 18g

Sugar: 2g

Serving Size:

Makes 2 servings.

Prep and Cook Time:

Prep Time: 10 minutes

Total Time: 25 minutes

Cook Time: 15 minutes

Ingredients:

- 2 salmon fillets
- 1 cup asparagus spears
- 1 tbsp olive oil
- 1 tsp garlic powder
- Salt and pepper to taste

Instructions:

1. Preheat a grill or skillet. Coat salmon and asparagus with olive oil, garlic powder, salt, and pepper.

2. Grill salmon for 4–5 minutes per side and asparagus until tender. Serve together.

---

6. Chickpea and Veggie Stir-Fry

Nutritional Information (Per Serving):

Calories: 280

Carbohydrates: 36g

Protein: 10g

Fiber: 8g

Fat: 10g

Sugar: 6g

Serving Size:

Makes 2 servings.

Prep and Cook Time:

Prep Time: 10 minutes

Cook Time: 10 minutes

Total Time: 20 minutes

Ingredients:

- 1 cup cooked chickpeas
- 1 cup broccoli florets
- ½ cup sliced carrots
- 1 tbsp soy sauce
- 1 tbsp olive oil

Instructions:

1. Heat olive oil in a skillet and sauté broccoli and carrots for 5 minutes.

2. Add chickpeas and soy sauce. Cook for 5 more minutes. Serve warm.

---

7. Tuna Salad Lettuce Wraps

Nutritional Information (Per Serving):

Calories: 220g

Protein: 20g

Fat: 12g

Carbohydrates: 6g

Fiber: 2g

Sugar: 1g

Serving Size:

Makes 2 wraps.

Prep and Cook Time:

Prep Time: 10 minutes

Cook Time: 0 minutes

Total Time: 10 minutes

Ingredients:

- 1 can tuna in water, drained
- 1 tbsp mayonnaise

- 1 tsp Dijon mustard
- 2 large lettuce leaves
- ¼ cup diced celery

Instructions:

1. Mix tuna, mayonnaise, mustard, and celery in a bowl.

2. Scoop mixture into lettuce leaves and serve.

---

8. Shrimp and Avocado Bowl

Nutritional Information (Per Serving):

Calories: 320

Protein: 22g

Fat: 15g

Carbohydrates: 22g

Fiber: 5g

Sugar: 2g

Serving Size:

Makes 2 bowls.

Prep and Cook Time:

Prep Time: 10 minutes

Cook Time: 10 minutes

Total Time: 20 minutes

Ingredients:

- 1 cup cooked shrimp
- 1 cup cooked brown rice
- ½ avocado, diced
- ½ cup cherry tomatoes, halved
- 1 tbsp olive oil

Instructions:

1. Combine shrimp, rice, avocado, and cherry tomatoes in a bowl.

2. Drizzle with olive oil and serve.

---

9. Grilled Vegetable Panini

Nutritional Information (Per Serving):

Calories: 280

Protein: 10g

Fat: 8g

Carbohydrates: 42g

Fiber: 6g

Sugar: 5g

Serving Size:

Makes 1 panini.

Prep and Cook Time:

Prep Time: 10 minutes

Cook Time: 5 minutes

Total Time: 15 minutes

Ingredients:

- 2 slices whole-grain bread
- ¼ cup grilled zucchini slices
- ¼ cup grilled bell peppers
- 1 slice mozzarella cheese
- 1 tsp pesto

Instructions:

1. Assemble panini with zucchini, peppers, mozzarella, and pesto.

2. Grill until bread is crispy and cheese is melted.

10. Caprese Chicken Salad

Nutritional Information (Per Serving):

Calories: 290

Protein: 25g

Fat: 18g

Carbohydrates: 8g

Fiber: 2g

Sugar: 4g

Serving Size:

Makes 2 servings.

Prep and Cook Time:

Prep Time: 10 minutes

Cook Time: 5 minutes

Total Time: 15 minutes

Ingredients:

- 2 cups mixed greens
- 1 grilled chicken breast, sliced
- ½ cup cherry tomatoes, halved
- ¼ cup fresh mozzarella balls
- 1 tbsp olive oil
- 1 tbsp balsamic glaze

Instructions:

1. Combine greens, chicken, tomatoes, and mozzarella in a bowl.

2. Drizzle with olive oil and balsamic glaze. Toss gently and serve.

---

11. Greek-Inspired Turkey Meatballs with Cucumber Salad

Nutritional Information (Per Serving):

Calories: 320

Protein: 25g

Fat: 15g

Carbohydrates: 18g

Fiber: 3g

Sugar: 4g

Serving Size:

Makes 4 meatballs.

Prep and Cook Time:

Prep Time: 10 minutes

Cook Time: 15 minutes

Total Time: 25 minutes

Ingredients:

- 8 oz ground turkey
- 1 tsp dried oregano
- 1 clove garlic, minced
- ½ cucumber, sliced
- ¼ cup Greek yogurt
- 1 tsp lemon juice

Instructions:

1. Mix turkey, oregano, and garlic. Form into meatballs and bake at 375°F (190°C) for 15 minutes.

2. Serve with cucumber slices and a dollop of yogurt mixed with lemon juice.

---

12. Baked Falafel Bowl with Tahini Dressing

Nutritional Information (Per Serving):

Calories: 300

Carbohydrates: 36g

Protein: 12g

Fiber: 8g

Fat: 14g

Sugar: 3g

Serving Size:

Makes 2 servings.

Prep and Cook Time:

Prep Time: 10 minutes

Total Time: 30 minutes

Cook Time: 20 minutes

Ingredients:

- 6 baked falafel balls (store-bought or homemade)
- 1 cup cooked quinoa
- ½ cup shredded lettuce
- ¼ cup cherry tomatoes, halved
- 1 tbsp tahini dressing

Instructions:

1. Assemble falafel, quinoa, lettuce, and tomatoes in a bowl.

2. Drizzle with tahini dressing and serve.

---

13. Eggplant and Chickpea Curry

Nutritional Information (Per Serving):

Calories: 280

Protein: 10g

Fat: 12g

Carbohydrates: 36g

Fiber: 10g

Sugar: 6g

Serving Size:

Makes 2 servings.

Prep and Cook Time:

Prep Time: 10 minutes

Cook Time: 20 minutes

Total Time: 30 minutes

Ingredients:

- 1 small eggplant, diced
- 1 cup chickpeas, cooked
- 1 cup coconut milk
- 1 tbsp curry powder
- 1 tbsp olive oil

Instructions:

1. Heat olive oil in a pan and sauté eggplant until soft.
2. Add chickpeas, coconut milk, and curry powder. Simmer for 15 minutes. Serve warm.

---

14. Spinach and Ricotta Stuffed Peppers

Nutritional Information (Per Serving):

Calories: 260

Protein: 14g

Fat: 12g

Carbohydrates: 24g

Fiber: 6g

Sugar: 8g

Serving Size:

Makes 2 stuffed peppers.

Prep and Cook Time:

Prep Time: 10 minutes

Cook Time: 25 minutes

Total Time: 35 minutes

Ingredients:

- 2 bell peppers, halved and deseeded
- 1 cup fresh spinach, chopped
- ½ cup ricotta cheese
- ¼ cup shredded mozzarella

Instructions:

1. Preheat oven to 375°F (190°C).

2. Mix spinach and ricotta, then fill peppers. Top with mozzarella.

3. Bake for 25 minutes or until tender. Serve warm.

---

15. Shrimp and Zoodles Stir-Fry

Nutritional Information (Per Serving):

Calories: 250

Protein: 22g

Fat: 10g

Carbohydrates: 18g

Fiber: 4g

Sugar: 5g

Serving Size:

Makes 2 servings.

Prep and Cook Time:

Prep Time: 10 minutes

Cook Time: 10 minutes

Total Time: 20 minutes

Ingredients:

- 1 cup zucchini noodles
- 1 cup cooked shrimp
- ½ cup sliced bell peppers
- 1 tbsp soy sauce
- 1 tsp sesame oil

Instructions:

1. Heat sesame oil in a skillet and sauté zucchini noodles and bell peppers for 5 minutes.

2. Add shrimp and soy sauce. Stir until heated through.

---

16. Sweet Potato and Lentil Salad

Nutritional Information (Per Serving):

Calories: 300

Protein: 14g

Fat: 8g

Carbohydrates: 45g

Fiber: 10g

Sugar: 8g

Serving Size:

Makes 2 servings.

Prep and Cook Time:

Prep Time: 10 minutes

Cook Time: 20 minutes

Total Time: 30 minutes

Ingredients:

- 1 medium sweet potato, cubed and roasted
- 1 cup cooked lentils
- 2 cups arugula
- 1 tbsp olive oil
- 1 tsp apple cider vinegar

Instructions:

1. Combine sweet potato, lentils, and arugula in a bowl.

2. Drizzle with olive oil and apple cider vinegar. Toss and serve.

---

17. Grilled Tuna and Asparagus Plate

Nutritional Information (Per Serving):

Calories: 320

Carbohydrates: 8g

Protein: 25g

Fiber: 3g

Fat: 12g

Sugar: 1g

Serving Size:

Makes 2 servings.

Prep and Cook Time:

Prep Time: 10 minutes

Total Time: 20 minutes

Cook Time: 10 minutes

Ingredients:

- 1 tuna steak

- 1 cup asparagus spears

- 1 tbsp olive oil

- Salt and pepper to taste

Instructions:

1. Heat olive oil in a grill pan. Grill tuna for 3–4 minutes per side.

2. Cook asparagus in the same pan until tender. Serve together.

---

18. Chicken and Cucumber Noodle Salad

Nutritional Information (Per Serving):

Calories: 280

Carbohydrates: 24g

Protein: 22g

Fiber: 4g

Fat: 8g

Sugar: 3g

Serving Size:

Makes 2 servings.

Prep and Cook Time:

Prep Time: 10 minutes

Cook Time: 5 minutes

Total Time: 15 minutes

Ingredients:

- 1 cup shredded cooked chicken
- 1 cup cucumber noodles
- 1 tbsp peanut sauce
- 1 tbsp chopped peanuts

Instructions:

1. Toss chicken and cucumber noodles with peanut sauce.
2. Garnish with chopped peanuts and serve chilled.

---

19. Egg and Avocado Pita Pocket

Nutritional Information (Per Serving):

Calories: 260

Protein: 14g

Fat: 12g

Carbohydrates: 26g

Fiber: 5g

Sugar: 2g

Serving Size:

Makes 1 pocket.

Prep and Cook Time:

Prep Time: 5 minutes

Cook Time: 5 minutes

Total Time: 10 minutes

Ingredients:

- 1 whole-grain pita pocket
- 1 boiled egg, sliced
- ¼ avocado, sliced
- 1 cup spinach

Instructions:

1. Fill pita pocket with spinach, egg, and avocado. Serve immediately.

20. Turkey and Avocado Lettuce Wraps

Nutritional Information (Per Serving):

Calories: 240

Protein: 20g

Fat: 14g

Carbohydrates: 8g

Fiber: 3g

Sugar: 1g

Serving Size:

Makes 2 wraps.

Prep and Cook Time:

Prep Time: 5 minutes

Cook Time: 0 minutes

Total Time: 5 minutes

Ingredients:

- 4 large lettuce leaves
- 4 oz turkey breast, sliced
- ½ avocado, sliced
- 1 tbsp Dijon mustard

Instructions:

1. Lay out lettuce leaves and spread mustard on each.
2. Layer turkey and avocado slices. Wrap tightly and serve.

---

21. Warm Barley and Roasted Veggie Salad

Nutritional Information (Per Serving):

Calories: 320

Protein: 10g

Fat: 12g

Carbohydrates: 42g

Fiber: 7g

Sugar: 6g

Serving Size:

Makes 2 servings.

Prep and Cook Time:

Prep Time: 10 minutes

Total Time: 35 minutes

Cook Time: 25 minutes

Ingredients:

- ½ cup cooked barley
- 1 cup roasted vegetables (zucchini, bell peppers, carrots)
- 2 cups mixed greens
- 1 tbsp olive oil
- 1 tsp balsamic vinegar

Instructions:

1. Combine barley, roasted vegetables, and greens in a bowl.

2. Drizzle with olive oil and balsamic vinegar. Toss and serve warm.

---

22. Grilled Halloumi and Vegetable Skewers

Nutritional Information (Per Serving):

Calories: 280

Carbohydrates: 12g

Protein: 15g

Fiber: 4g

Fat: 18g

Sugar: 4g

Serving Size:

Makes 4 skewers.

Prep and Cook Time:

Prep Time: 10 minutes

Total Time: 20 minutes

Cook Time: 10 minutes

Ingredients:

- 4 oz halloumi cheese, cubed
- 1 cup zucchini slices
- 1 cup cherry tomatoes
- 1 tbsp olive oil

Instructions:

1. Thread halloumi, zucchini, and cherry tomatoes onto skewers.

2. Brush with olive oil and grill for 10 minutes, turning occasionally.

---

23. Baked Cod with Lemon and Herbs

Nutritional Information (Per Serving):

Calories: 220

Carbohydrates: 6g

Protein: 25g

Fiber: 2g

Fat: 8g

Sugar: 1g

Serving Size:

Makes 2 servings.

Prep and Cook Time:

Prep Time: 5 minutes

Total Time: 20 minutes

Cook Time: 15 minutes

Ingredients:

- 2 cod fillets

- 1 tbsp lemon juice

- 1 tbsp olive oil

- 1 tsp dried thyme

Instructions:

1. Preheat oven to 375°F (190°C).

2. Brush cod with olive oil and lemon juice, then sprinkle with thyme.

3. Bake for 15 minutes or until flaky. Serve with steamed veggies.

---

24. Veggie and Hummus Stuffed Pita

Nutritional Information (Per Serving):

Calories: 270

Protein: 10g

Fat: 10g

Carbohydrates: 38g

Fiber: 8g

Sugar: 3g

Serving Size:

Makes 1 pita.

Prep and Cook Time:

Prep Time: 5 minutes

Cook Time: 0 minutes

Total Time: 5 minutes

Ingredients:

- 1 whole-grain pita pocket
- 3 tbsp hummus
- ¼ cup shredded carrots
- ¼ cup sliced cucumber
- ¼ cup spinach

Instructions:

1. Spread hummus inside the pita.
2. Stuff with carrots, cucumber, and spinach. Serve immediately.

---

25. Asian-Inspired Cabbage Slaw with Chicken

Nutritional Information (Per Serving):

Calories: 250

Protein: 20g

Fat: 10g

Carbohydrates: 15g

Fiber: 5g

Sugar: 4g

Serving Size:

Makes 2 servings.

Prep and Cook Time:

Prep Time: 10 minutes

Total Time: 15 minutes

Cook Time: 5 minutes

Ingredients:

- 2 cups shredded cabbage
- 1 cup cooked shredded chicken
- 1 tbsp sesame oil
- 1 tsp soy sauce
- 1 tsp rice vinegar

Instructions:

1. Toss cabbage and chicken with sesame oil, soy sauce, and rice vinegar.

2. Serve chilled or at room temperature.

---

26. Black Bean and Corn Salad

Nutritional Information (Per Serving):

Calories: 280

Carbohydrates: 42g

Protein: 10g

Fiber: 10g

Fat: 8g

Sugar: 6g

Serving Size:

Makes 2 servings.

Prep and Cook Time:

Prep Time: 10 minutes

Total Time: 10 minutes

Cook Time: 0 minutes

Ingredients:

- 1 cup black beans, rinsed
- 1 cup corn kernels
- ¼ cup diced red onion
- 1 tbsp olive oil
- 1 tbsp lime juice

Instructions:

1. Combine black beans, corn, and red onion in a bowl.

2. Drizzle with olive oil and lime juice. Toss and serve.

---

27. Mediterranean Tuna Salad

Nutritional Information (Per Serving):

Calories: 260

Protein: 20g

Fat: 12g

Carbohydrates: 14g

Fiber: 3g

Sugar: 2g

Serving Size:

Makes 2 servings.

Prep and Cook Time:

Prep Time: 10 minutes

Cook Time: 0 minutes

Total Time: 10 minutes

Ingredients:

- 1 can tuna in olive oil, drained

- ¼ cup diced cucumber

- ¼ cup diced tomato

- 1 tbsp feta cheese

- 1 tsp lemon juice

Instructions:

1. Mix tuna, cucumber, tomato, and feta in a bowl.

2. Drizzle with lemon juice and serve.

---

28. Sweet Potato and Kale Buddha Bowl

Nutritional Information (Per Serving):

Calories: 290

Protein: 12g

Fat: 10g

Fiber: 8g

Carbohydrates: 40g

Sugar: 5g

Serving Size:

Makes 2 servings.

Prep and Cook Time:

Prep Time: 10 minutes

Total Time: 30 minutes

Cook Time: 20 minutes

Ingredients:

- 1 medium sweet potato, roasted
- ½ cup cooked quinoa
- 1 cup cooked kale
- 1 tbsp tahini dressing

Instructions:

1. Combine sweet potato, kale, and quinoa in a bowl.
2. Drizzle with tahini dressing. Serve warm or chilled.

---

29. Grilled Shrimp Caesar Salad

Nutritional Information (Per Serving):

Calories: 270

Carbohydrates: 10g

Protein: 22g

Fiber: 2g

Fat: 14g

Sugar: 1g

Serving Size:

Makes 2 servings.

Prep and Cook Time:

Prep Time: 10 minutes

Total Time: 20 minutes

Cook Time: 10 minutes

Ingredients:

- 1 cup grilled shrimp
- 2 cups romaine lettuce

69

- 2 tbsp Caesar dressing
- 1 tbsp grated Parmesan cheese

Instructions:

1. Toss lettuce with Caesar dressing.

2. Top with shrimp and Parmesan. Serve immediately.

---

30. Warm Lentil and Arugula Salad

Nutritional Information (Per Serving):

Calories: 280

Carbohydrates: 35g

Protein: 14g

Fiber: 10g

Fat: 8g

Sugar: 3g

Serving Size:

Makes 2 servings.

Prep and Cook Time:

Prep Time: 10 minutes

Total Time: 20 minutes

Cook Time: 10 minutes

Ingredients:

- 1 cup cooked lentils
- 1 tbsp olive oil
- 2 cups arugula
- 1 tsp Dijon mustard

Instructions:

1. Heat lentils and toss with arugula, olive oil, and Dijon mustard.

2. Serve warm as a main or side dish.

30 Dinners That Satisfy Your Tastebuds and Your Metabolism

1. Lemon Herb Chicken with Roasted Brussels Sprouts

Nutritional Information (Per Serving):

Calories: 320

Protein: 35g

Fat: 12g

Carbohydrates: 12g

Fiber: 4g

Sugar: 2g

Serving Size:

Makes 2 servings.

Prep and Cook Time:

Prep Time: 10 minutes

Cook Time: 25 minutes

Total Time: 35 minutes

Ingredients:

- 2 boneless, skinless chicken breasts
- 2 cups Brussels sprouts, halved
- 1 tbsp olive oil
- 1 tsp dried oregano
- 1 tsp lemon zest
- Salt and pepper to taste

Instructions:

1. Preheat oven to 400°F (200°C).
2. Toss Brussels sprouts with olive oil, salt, and pepper. Place on a baking sheet.
3. Season chicken with oregano, lemon zest, salt, and pepper. Add to the sheet.
4. Roast for 25 minutes or until chicken is cooked through. Serve warm.

---

2. Garlic Shrimp with Zucchini Noodles

Nutritional Information (Per Serving):

Calories: 280

Protein: 22g

Fat: 10g

Fiber: 4g

Carbohydrates: 15g

Sugar: 4g

Serving Size:

Makes 2 servings.

Prep and Cook Time:

Prep Time: 10 minutes

Total Time: 20 minutes

Cook Time: 10 minutes

Ingredients:

- 1 lb shrimp, peeled and deveined
- 2 cups zucchini noodles
- 2 tbsp olive oil
- 2 garlic cloves, minced
- 1 tbsp lemon juice

Instructions:

1. Heat olive oil in a skillet. Sauté garlic until fragrant.

2. Add shrimp and cook until pink. Stir in zucchini noodles and lemon juice. Serve warm.

---

3. Baked Salmon with Dill and Asparagus

Nutritional Information (Per Serving):

Calories: 310

Carbohydrates: 8g

Protein: 28g

Fiber: 2g

Fat: 18g

Sugar: 1g

Serving Size:

Makes 2 servings.

Prep and Cook Time:

Prep Time: 10 minutes

Total Time: 25 minutes

Cook Time: 15 minutes

Ingredients:

- 2 salmon fillets
- 1 cup asparagus spears
- 1 tbsp olive oil
- 1 tsp dried dill
- 1 lemon wedge

Instructions:

1. Preheat oven to 375°F (190°C).

2. Place salmon and asparagus on a baking sheet. Drizzle with olive oil and sprinkle with dill.

3. Bake for 15 minutes or until salmon is cooked through. Serve with a squeeze of lemon.

---

4. Turkey Meatball Zoodles

Nutritional Information (Per Serving):

Calories: 330

Protein: 28g

Fat: 10g

Carbohydrates: 25g

Fiber: 5g

Sugar: 6g

Serving Size:

Makes 4 meatballs and 1 cup zoodles per serving.

Prep and Cook Time:

Prep Time: 15 minutes

Cook Time: 20 minutes

Total Time: 35 minutes

Ingredients:

- 8 oz ground turkey
- 1 egg
- ½ cup breadcrumbs
- 1 tsp Italian seasoning
- 2 cups zucchini noodles
- 1 cup marinara sauce

Instructions:

1. Mix turkey, egg, breadcrumbs, and seasoning. Form into meatballs.

2. Bake at 375°F (190°C) for 20 minutes.

3. Heat marinara sauce and zucchini noodles in a skillet. Serve meatballs over zoodles.

---

5. Quinoa-Stuffed Bell Peppers

Nutritional Information (Per Serving):

Calories: 280

Protein: 12g

Fat: 8g

Carbohydrates: 42g

Fiber: 6g

Sugar: 6g

Serving Size:

Makes 2 stuffed peppers.

Prep and Cook Time:

Prep Time: 10 minutes

Cook Time: 30 minutes

Total Time: 40 minutes

Ingredients:

- 2 large bell peppers, halved and deseeded
- 1 cup cooked quinoa
- ½ cup black beans, rinsed
- ¼ cup diced tomatoes
- 1 tbsp olive oil

Instructions:

1. Preheat oven to 375°F (190°C).

2. Mix quinoa, black beans, and tomatoes. Stuff peppers with the mixture.

3. Drizzle with olive oil and bake for 30 minutes. Serve warm.

---

6. Herb-Crusted Cod with Steamed Vegetables

Nutritional Information (Per Serving):

Calories: 270

Protein: 30g

Fat: 10g

Carbohydrates: 12g

Fiber: 3g

Sugar: 2g

Serving Size:

Makes 2 servings.

Prep and Cook Time:

Prep Time: 10 minutes

Cook Time: 15 minutes

Total Time: 25 minutes

Ingredients:

- 2 cod fillets
- 1 tsp dried parsley
- 1 tsp garlic powder
- 1 cup broccoli florets
- 1 cup sliced carrots

Instructions:

1. Season cod with parsley, garlic powder, salt, and pepper.

2. Bake at 375°F (190°C) for 15 minutes.

3. Steam broccoli and carrots. Serve cod with vegetables.

7. Chicken Stir-Fry with Snow Peas

Nutritional Information (Per Serving):

Calories: 300

Protein: 26g

Fat: 12g

Carbohydrates: 18g

Fiber: 4g

Sugar: 5g

Serving Size:

Makes 2 servings.

Prep and Cook Time:

Prep Time: 10 minutes

Cook Time: 15 minutes

Total Time: 25 minutes

Ingredients:

- 1 chicken breast, sliced
- 1 cup snow peas
- 1 cup sliced mushrooms
- 1 tbsp soy sauce
- 1 tbsp sesame oil

Instructions:

1. Heat sesame oil in a skillet. Cook chicken until browned.

2. Add snow peas, mushrooms, and soy sauce. Stir-fry until vegetables are tender. Serve warm.

---

8. Lentil and Sweet Potato Curry

Nutritional Information (Per Serving):

Calories: 320

Protein: 14g

Fat: 10g

Carbohydrates: 45g

Fiber: 8g

Sugar: 8g

Serving Size:

Makes 2 servings.

Prep and Cook Time:

Prep Time: 10 minutes

Cook Time: 25 minutes

Total Time: 35 minutes

Ingredients:

- 1 cup cooked lentils
- 1 medium sweet potato, diced

- 1 cup coconut milk
- 1 tbsp curry powder

Instructions:

1. Sauté sweet potato in a pot until soft.

2. Add lentils, coconut milk, and curry powder. Simmer for 15 minutes. Serve warm.

---

9. Steak and Cauliflower Mash

Nutritional Information (Per Serving):

Calories: 340

Carbohydrates: 12g

Protein: 28g

Fiber: 4g

Fat: 18g

Sugar: 2g

Serving Size:

Makes 2 servings.

Prep and Cook Time:

Prep Time: 10 minutes

Total Time: 30 minutes

Cook Time: 20 minutes

Ingredients:

- 2 sirloin steaks
- 1 tbsp butter
- 2 cups cauliflower florets
- Salt and pepper to taste

Instructions:

1. Grill steaks to desired doneness.

2. Boil cauliflower until tender, then mash with butter, salt, and pepper. Serve together.

---

10. Baked Eggplant Parmesan

Nutritional Information (Per Serving):

Calories: 280

Protein: 14g

Fat: 12g

Carbohydrates: 28g

Fiber: 6g

Sugar: 6g

Serving Size:

Makes 2 servings.

Prep and Cook Time:

Prep Time: 15 minutes

Cook Time: 25 minutes

Total Time: 40 minutes

Ingredients:

- 1 medium eggplant, sliced
- ½ cup marinara sauce
- ¼ cup shredded mozzarella
- 1 tbsp olive oil

Instructions:

1. Preheat oven to 375°F (190°C).
2. Brush eggplant slices with olive oil and bake for 15 minutes.
3. Top with marinara and mozzarella. Bake for another 10 minutes. Serve warm.

---

11. Balsamic Glazed Chicken with Roasted Vegetables

Nutritional Information (Per Serving):

Calories: 330

Protein: 30g

Fat: 12g

Carbohydrates: 20g

Fiber: 5g

Sugar: 8g

Serving Size:

Makes 2 servings.

Prep and Cook Time:

Prep Time: 10 minutes

Cook Time: 30 minutes

Total Time: 40 minutes

Ingredients:

- 2 boneless chicken breasts
- 1 cup broccoli florets
- 1 cup diced carrots
- 2 tbsp balsamic vinegar
- 1 tbsp olive oil

Instructions:

1. Preheat oven to 375°F (190°C).
2. Coat chicken and vegetables with olive oil and balsamic vinegar. Place on a baking sheet.
3. Bake for 30 minutes, turning chicken halfway through. Serve warm.

12. Grilled Pork Chops with Apple and Cabbage Slaw

Nutritional Information (Per Serving):

Calories: 350

Protein: 28g

Fat: 15g

Carbohydrates: 25g

Fiber: 5g

Sugar: 10g

Serving Size:

Makes 2 servings.

Prep and Cook Time:

Prep Time: 10 minutes

Cook Time: 20 minutes

Total Time: 30 minutes

Ingredients:

- 2 pork chops
- 1 cup shredded cabbage
- 1 small apple, thinly sliced
- 1 tbsp apple cider vinegar
- 1 tbsp olive oil

Instructions:

1. Season pork chops with salt and pepper and grill until cooked through.

2. Toss cabbage and apple with apple cider vinegar and olive oil. Serve with pork chops.

---

13. Spaghetti Squash with Turkey Bolognese

Nutritional Information (Per Serving):

Calories: 320

Protein: 25g

Fat: 12g

Carbohydrates: 28g

Fiber: 7g

Sugar: 10g

Serving Size:

Makes 2 servings.

Prep and Cook Time:

Prep Time: 15 minutes

Cook Time: 25 minutes

Total Time: 40 minutes

Ingredients:

- 1 small spaghetti squash, halved and roasted
- 1 cup ground turkey
- 1 cup marinara sauce
- 1 tsp Italian seasoning

Instructions:

1. Roast squash at 375°F (190°C) for 25 minutes. Scrape out strands with a fork.

2. Cook turkey in a skillet, add marinara sauce and seasoning. Serve over squash.

---

14. Coconut Curry Chicken with Cauliflower Rice

Nutritional Information (Per Serving):

Calories: 340

Protein: 28g

Fat: 15g

Carbohydrates: 20g

Fiber: 5g

Sugar: 6g

Serving Size:

Makes 2 servings.

Prep and Cook Time:

Prep Time: 10 minutes

Cook Time: 20 minutes

Total Time: 30 minutes

Ingredients:

- 1 chicken breast, cubed
- 1 cup coconut milk
- 1 tbsp curry powder
- 1 cup cauliflower rice

Instructions:

1. Cook chicken in a skillet until browned. Add coconut milk and curry powder. Simmer for 10 minutes.
2. Serve over cauliflower rice.

---

15. Seared Tuna with Avocado Salsa

Nutritional Information (Per Serving):

Calories: 310

Protein: 32g

Fat: 16g

Sugar: 2g

Carbohydrates: 8g

Fiber: 4g

Serving Size:

Makes 2 servings.

Prep and Cook Time:

Prep Time: 10 minutes

Cook Time: 5 minutes

Total Time: 15 minutes

Ingredients:

- 2 tuna steaks
- 1 avocado, diced
- ½ cup diced tomatoes
- 1 tbsp lime juice

Instructions:

1. Sear tuna steaks in a skillet for 2 minutes per side.
2. Mix avocado, tomatoes, and lime juice. Serve salsa over tuna.

---

16. Beef and Broccoli Stir-Fry

Nutritional Information (Per Serving):

Calories: 320

Protein: 28g

Fat: 12g

Carbohydrates: 20g

Fiber: 4g

Sugar: 6g

Serving Size:

Makes 2 servings.

Prep and Cook Time:

Prep Time: 10 minutes

Cook Time: 15 minutes

Total Time: 25 minutes

Ingredients:

- 1 cup beef strips
- 2 cups broccoli florets
- 1 tbsp soy sauce
- 1 tsp sesame oil

Instructions:

1. Heat sesame oil in a skillet. Cook beef until browned.

2. Add broccoli and soy sauce. Stir-fry until tender. Serve warm.

---

17. Eggplant and Chickpea Stew

Nutritional Information (Per Serving):

Calories: 280

Carbohydrates: 40g

Protein: 10g

Fiber: 10g

Fat: 8g

Sugar: 6g

Serving Size:

Makes 2 servings.

Prep and Cook Time:

Prep Time: 10 minutes

Total Time: 35 minutes

Cook Time: 25 minutes

Ingredients:

- 1 medium eggplant, diced

- 1 cup chickpeas, cooked

- 1 cup diced tomatoes

- 1 tsp smoked paprika

Instructions:

1. Sauté eggplant in olive oil until soft.

2. Add chickpeas, tomatoes, and paprika. Simmer for 20 minutes. Serve warm.

---

18. Herb-Roasted Chicken Thighs with Green Beans

Nutritional Information (Per Serving):

Calories: 330

Carbohydrates: 12g

Protein: 28g

Fiber: 4g

Fat: 15g

Sugar: 2g

Serving Size:

Makes 2 servings.

Prep and Cook Time:

Prep Time: 10 minutes

Total Time: 35 minutes

Cook Time: 25 minutes

Ingredients:

- 2 chicken thighs

- 1 tbsp olive oil

- 1 cup green beans

- 1 tsp garlic powder

Instructions:

1. Season chicken with olive oil and garlic powder. Roast at 375°F (190°C) for 25 minutes.

2. Steam green beans and serve with chicken.

19. Turkey and Sweet Potato Shepherd's Pie

Nutritional Information (Per Serving):

Calories: 310

Carbohydrates: 35g

Protein: 22g

Fiber: 6g

Fat: 10g

Sugar: 8g

Serving Size:

Makes 2 servings.

Prep and Cook Time:

Prep Time: 10 minutes

Cook Time: 30 minutes

Total Time: 40 minutes

Ingredients:

- 1 cup ground turkey

- 1 medium sweet potato, mashed

- 1 cup mixed vegetables

- 1 tsp olive oil

Instructions:

1. Cook turkey in a skillet. Add mixed vegetables.

2. Layer turkey and vegetables in a baking dish. Top with mashed sweet potato.

3. Bake at 375°F (190°C) for 20 minutes.

20. Baked Tilapia with Spinach and Garlic

Nutritional Information (Per Serving):

Calories: 280

Protein: 28g

Fat: 10g

Carbohydrates: 10g

Fiber: 2g

Sugar: 1g

Serving Size:

Makes 2 servings.

Prep and Cook Time:

Prep Time: 10 minutes

Cook Time: 20 minutes

Total Time: 30 minutes

Ingredients:

- 2 tilapia fillets

- 2 cups fresh spinach

- 2 garlic cloves, minced

- 1 tbsp olive oil

Instructions:

1. Preheat oven to 375°F (190°C).

2. Place tilapia on a baking sheet. Drizzle with olive oil and sprinkle with garlic.

3. Bake for 15–20 minutes. Sauté spinach in olive oil and serve with fish.

---

21. Roasted Chicken and Vegetable Tray Bake

Nutritional Information (Per Serving):

Calories: 320

Carbohydrates: 20g

Protein: 28g

Fiber: 6g

Fat: 12g

Sugar: 4g

Serving Size:

Makes 2 servings.

Prep and Cook Time:

Prep Time: 10 minutes

Total Time: 40 minutes

Cook Time: 30 minutes

Ingredients:

- 2 chicken thighs
- 1 cup diced sweet potatoes
- 1 cup zucchini slices
- 1 tbsp olive oil
- 1 tsp rosemary

Instructions:

1. Preheat oven to 400°F (200°C).

2. Arrange chicken, sweet potatoes, and zucchini on a baking sheet.

3. Drizzle with olive oil, sprinkle with rosemary, and bake for 30 minutes.

---

22. Teriyaki Salmon with Stir-Fried Bok Choy

Nutritional Information (Per Serving):

Calories: 340

Carbohydrates: 20g

Protein: 28g

Fiber: 4g

Fat: 14g

Sugar: 8g

Serving Size:

Makes 2 servings.

Prep and Cook Time:

Prep Time: 10 minutes

Total Time: 25 minutes

Cook Time: 15 minutes

Ingredients:

- 2 salmon fillets
- 2 tbsp teriyaki sauce
- 2 cups bok choy, chopped
- 1 tbsp sesame oil

Instructions:

1. Brush salmon with teriyaki sauce and bake at 375°F (190°C) for 12–15 minutes.

2. Heat sesame oil in a skillet and stir-fry bok choy for 5 minutes. Serve together.

23. Stuffed Portobello Mushrooms with Quinoa and Spinach

Nutritional Information (Per Serving):

Calories: 280

Carbohydrates: 30g

Protein: 12g

Fiber: 6g

Fat: 10g

Sugar: 4g

Serving Size:

Makes 2 stuffed mushrooms.

Prep and Cook Time:

Prep Time: 10 minutes

Cook Time: 20 minutes

Total Time: 30 minutes

Ingredients:

- 2 large Portobello mushrooms
- 1 cup cooked quinoa
- 1 cup fresh spinach, chopped
- ¼ cup shredded Parmesan cheese

Instructions:

1. Preheat oven to 375°F (190°C).

2. Mix quinoa, spinach, and Parmesan. Stuff mushrooms with the mixture.

3. Bake for 20 minutes. Serve warm.

---

24. Turkey and Zucchini Skillet

Nutritional Information (Per Serving):

Calories: 300

Protein: 28g

Fat: 12g

Carbohydrates: 14g

Fiber: 3g

Sugar: 3g

Serving Size:

Makes 2 servings.

Prep and Cook Time:

Prep Time: 10 minutes

Cook Time: 15 minutes

Total Time: 25 minutes

Ingredients:

- 1 cup ground turkey
- 1 zucchini, diced
- ½ cup diced tomatoes
- 1 tbsp olive oil

Instructions:

1. Heat olive oil in a skillet. Cook turkey until browned.

2. Add zucchini and tomatoes. Cook until vegetables are tender. Serve warm.

---

25. Lemon Garlic Shrimp over Cauliflower Rice

Nutritional Information (Per Serving):

Calories: 290

Protein: 25g

Fat: 10g

Carbohydrates: 18g

Fiber: 4g

Sugar: 2g

Serving Size:

Makes 2 servings.

Prep and Cook Time:

Prep Time: 10 minutes

Cook Time: 10 minutes

Total Time: 20 minutes

Ingredients:

- 1 lb shrimp, peeled and deveined
- 2 cups cauliflower rice
- 1 tbsp olive oil
- 1 clove garlic, minced
- 1 tsp lemon juice

Instructions:

1. Heat olive oil in a skillet and sauté garlic. Add shrimp and cook until pink.

2. Stir in lemon juice. Serve over cauliflower rice.

---

26. Vegan Sweet Potato and Black Bean Chili

Nutritional Information (Per Serving):

Calories: 320

Protein: 12g

Fat: 8g

Carbohydrates: 50g

Fiber: 12g

Sugar: 8g

Serving Size:

Makes 2 servings.

Prep and Cook Time:

Prep Time: 10 minutes

Cook Time: 25 minutes

Total Time: 35 minutes

Ingredients:

- 1 medium sweet potato, diced
- 1 cup black beans, rinsed
- 1 cup diced tomatoes
- 1 tsp chili powder

Instructions:

1. Sauté sweet potato in a pot until soft.

2. Add black beans, tomatoes, and chili powder. Simmer for 20 minutes. Serve warm.

---

27. Beef and Cauliflower Shepherd's Pie

Nutritional Information (Per Serving):

Calories: 310

Protein: 25g

Fat: 12g

Carbohydrates: 18g

Fiber: 6g

Sugar: 3g

Serving Size:

Makes 2 servings.

Prep and Cook Time:

Prep Time: 10 minutes

Cook Time: 30 minutes

Total Time: 40 minutes

Ingredients:

- 1 cup ground beef
- 2 cups mashed cauliflower
- 1 cup mixed vegetables

Instructions:

1. Cook beef in a skillet. Add mixed vegetables and cook until tender.

2. Layer beef and vegetables in a baking dish. Top with mashed cauliflower. Bake at 375°F (190°C) for 20 minutes.

---

28. Honey Mustard Chicken with Steamed Broccoli

Nutritional Information (Per Serving):

Calories: 330

Protein: 30g

Fat: 12g

Carbohydrates: 18g

Fiber: 4g

Sugar: 6g

Serving Size:

Makes 2 servings.

Prep and Cook Time:

Prep Time: 10 minutes

Cook Time: 20 minutes

Total Time: 30 minutes

Ingredients:

- 2 chicken breasts
- 1 tbsp honey
- 1 tbsp Dijon mustard
- 2 cups broccoli florets

Instructions:

1. Mix honey and mustard. Brush over chicken. Bake at 375°F (190°C) for 20 minutes.

2. Steam broccoli and serve with chicken.

---

29. Cod with Lemon and Capers

Nutritional Information (Per Serving):

Calories: 280

Carbohydrates: 10g

Protein: 28g

Fiber: 2g

Fat: 10g

Sugar: 1g

Serving Size:

Makes 2 servings.

Prep and Cook Time:

Prep Time: 10 minutes

Total Time: 25 minutes

Cook Time: 15 minutes

Ingredients:

- 2 cod fillets

- 1 tbsp capers

- 1 tbsp olive oil

- 1 tsp lemon juice

Instructions:

1. Heat olive oil in a skillet. Cook cod for 3–4 minutes per side.

2. Add capers and lemon juice. Serve immediately.

---

30. Mediterranean Chickpea Stew

Nutritional Information (Per Serving):

Calories: 310

Fat: 10g

Protein: 12g

Carbohydrates: 42g

Fiber: 10g   Sugar: 6g

Serving Size:

Makes 2 servings.

Prep and Cook Time:

Prep Time: 10 minutes   Total Time: 35 minutes

Cook Time: 25 minutes

Ingredients:

- 1 cup chickpeas, cooked
- 1 cup diced tomatoes
- ½ cup chopped spinach
- 1 tsp dried oregano

Instructions:

1. Sauté chickpeas and tomatoes in olive oil. Add spinach and oregano.

2. Simmer for 10 minutes and serve warm.

20 Healthy Snacks to Curb Hunger Without Overeating

1. Greek Yogurt Dip with Veggie Sticks

Nutritional Information (Per Serving):

Calories: 120

Protein: 8g

Fat: 4g

Carbohydrates: 12g

Fiber: 3g

Sugar: 5g

Serving Size:

Makes 1 serving.

Prep and Cook Time:

Prep Time: 5 minutes

Cook Time: 0 minutes

Total Time: 5 minutes

Ingredients:

- ½ cup plain Greek yogurt
- 1 tsp lemon juice
- 1 tsp dried dill
- 1 cup carrot and celery sticks

Instructions:

1. Mix Greek yogurt, lemon juice, and dill in a bowl.

2. Serve with carrot and celery sticks for dipping.

---

2. Roasted Chickpeas

Nutritional Information (Per Serving):

Calories: 150

Protein: 6g

Fat: 5g

Carbohydrates: 20g

Fiber: 6g

Sugar: 1g

Serving Size:

Makes 2 servings.

Prep and Cook Time:

Prep Time: 5 minutes

Total Time: 35 minutes

Cook Time: 30 minutes

Ingredients:

- 1 cup cooked chickpeas
- 1 tsp paprika
- 1 tbsp olive oil

Instructions:

1. Preheat oven to 375°F (190°C).

2. Toss chickpeas with olive oil and paprika. Spread on a baking sheet.

3. Bake for 30 minutes, shaking halfway through. Let cool and enjoy.

---

3. Avocado and Cottage Cheese Boats

Nutritional Information (Per Serving):

Calories: 180

Carbohydrates: 8g

Protein: 10g

Fiber: 5g

Fat: 12g

Sugar: 2g

Serving Size:

Makes 1 serving.

Prep and Cook Time:

Prep Time: 5 minutes

Total Time: 5 minutes

Cook Time: 0 minutes

Ingredients:

- ½ avocado
- 1 pinch black pepper
- ¼ cup cottage cheese

Instructions:

1. Slice avocado in half and remove the pit.

2. Fill with cottage cheese and sprinkle with black pepper. Serve immediately.

---

4. Rice Cakes with Almond Butter and Banana

Nutritional Information (Per Serving):

Calories: 190

Protein: 5g

Fat: 8g

Carbohydrates: 25g

Fiber: 4g

Sugar: 10g

Serving Size:

Makes 1 serving.

Prep and Cook Time:

Prep Time: 5 minutes

Cook Time: 0 minutes

Total Time: 5 minutes

Ingredients:

- 2 rice cakes

- 1 tbsp almond butter

- ½ banana, sliced

Instructions:

1. Spread almond butter on rice cakes.

2. Top with banana slices. Serve immediately.

---

5. Hard-Boiled Egg and Guacamole

Nutritional Information (Per Serving):

Calories: 140

Protein: 7g

Fat: 10g

Carbohydrates: 5g

Fiber: 3g   Sugar: 1g

Serving Size:

Makes 1 serving.

Prep and Cook Time:

Prep Time: 5 minutes   Total Time: 15 minutes

Cook Time: 10 minutes (boiling time)

Ingredients:

- 1 hard-boiled egg   • 2 tbsp guacamole

Instructions:

1. Slice the egg in half and top with guacamole. Serve as a quick snack.

---

6. Cucumber and Hummus Bites

Nutritional Information (Per Serving):

Calories: 90   Carbohydrates: 10g

Protein: 3g   Fiber: 2g

Fat: 5g   Sugar: 2g

Serving Size:

Makes 1 serving.

Prep and Cook Time:

Prep Time: 5 minutes   Total Time: 5 minutes

Cook Time: 0 minutes

Ingredients:

- 1 small cucumber, sliced into rounds   • 2 tbsp hummus

Instructions:

1. Spread hummus on cucumber slices.

2. Arrange on a plate and serve immediately.

---

7. Trail Mix with Dark Chocolate

Nutritional Information (Per Serving):

Calories: 200

Protein: 6g

Fat: 12g

Carbohydrates: 20g

Fiber: 3g

Sugar: 8g

Serving Size:

Makes 1 serving.

Prep and Cook Time:

Prep Time: 5 minutes

Cook Time: 0 minutes

Total Time: 5 minutes

Ingredients:

- 1 tbsp almonds

- 1 tbsp walnuts

- 1 tbsp dried cranberries

- 1 tbsp dark chocolate chips

Instructions:

1. Mix all ingredients in a bowl. Serve as a portable snack.

---

8. Apple Slices with Peanut Butter

Nutritional Information (Per Serving):

Calories: 190

Protein: 5g

Fat: 8g

Carbohydrates: 28g

Fiber: 4g   Sugar: 18g

Serving Size:

Makes 1 serving.

Prep and Cook Time:

Prep Time: 5 minutes   Total Time: 5 minutes

Cook Time: 0 minutes

Ingredients:

- 1 small apple, sliced   • 1 tbsp peanut butter

Instructions:

1. Arrange apple slices on a plate.

2. Serve with peanut butter for dipping.

---

9. Edamame with Sea Salt

Nutritional Information (Per Serving):

Calories: 120   Carbohydrates: 12g

Protein: 10g   Fiber: 5g

Fat: 4g   Sugar: 2g

Serving Size:

Makes 1 serving.

Prep and Cook Time:

Prep Time: 5 minutes   Total Time: 10 minutes

Cook Time: 5 minutes

Ingredients:

- 1 cup edamame, in pods   • 1 pinch sea salt

Instructions:

1. Boil edamame for 5 minutes.

2. Drain, sprinkle with sea salt, and serve.

---

10. Baked Kale Chips

Nutritional Information (Per Serving):

Calories: 90

Protein: 3g

Fat: 5g

Carbohydrates: 10g

Fiber: 2g

Sugar: 1g

Serving Size:

Makes 1 serving.

Prep and Cook Time:

Prep Time: 5 minutes

Cook Time: 10 minutes

Total Time: 15 minutes

Ingredients:

- 1 cup kale leaves, torn into pieces
- 1 tbsp olive oil
- 1 pinch sea salt

Instructions:

1. Preheat oven to 375°F (190°C).

2. Toss kale with olive oil and sea salt. Spread on a baking sheet.

3. Bake for 10 minutes or until crispy. Serve immediately.

---

11. Berry and Chia Seed Parfait

Nutritional Information (Per Serving):

Calories: 180

Carbohydrates: 30g

Protein: 6g

Fiber: 8g

Fat: 4g

Sugar: 12g

Serving Size:

Makes 1 serving.

Prep and Cook Time:

Prep Time: 5 minutes

Total Time: 5 minutes

Cook Time: 0 minutes

Ingredients:

- ½ cup plain Greek yogurt
- 1 tsp chia seeds
- ½ cup mixed berries (blueberries, raspberries, strawberries)
- 1 tsp honey

Instructions:

1. Layer Greek yogurt, berries, and chia seeds in a glass.

2. Drizzle with honey and serve immediately.

12. Turkey Roll-Ups with Spinach

Nutritional Information (Per Serving):

Calories: 120

Carbohydrates: 2g

Protein: 14g

Fiber: 1g

Fat: 4g

Sugar: 1g

Serving Size:

Makes 1 serving.

Prep and Cook Time:

Prep Time: 5 minutes

Total Time: 5 minutes

Cook Time: 0 minutes

Ingredients:

- 4 slices turkey breast

- 1 cup fresh spinach

- 1 tsp mustard (optional)

Instructions:

1. Spread mustard on turkey slices.

2. Place spinach leaves on top and roll tightly. Serve immediately.

---

13. Almond Butter and Celery Sticks

Nutritional Information (Per Serving):

Calories: 160

Carbohydrates: 10g

Protein: 4g

Fiber: 4g

Fat: 12g

Sugar: 4g

Serving Size:

Makes 1 serving.

Prep and Cook Time:

Prep Time: 5 minutes

Total Time: 5 minutes

Cook Time: 0 minutes

Ingredients:

- 3 celery sticks

- 1 tbsp almond butter

Instructions:

1. Spread almond butter onto celery sticks.

2. Arrange on a plate and serve.

---

14. Spiced Almonds

Nutritional Information (Per Serving):

Calories: 200

Carbohydrates: 8g

Protein: 6g

Fiber: 4g

Fat: 16g

Sugar: 2g

Serving Size:

Makes 1 serving.

Prep and Cook Time:

Prep Time: 5 minutes

Total Time: 15 minutes

Cook Time: 10 minutes

Ingredients:

- ¼ cup almonds
- ½ tsp olive oil
- ½ tsp smoked paprika

Instructions:

1. Toss almonds with olive oil and paprika.

2. Roast in the oven at 350°F (175°C) for 10 minutes. Let cool before serving.

---

15. Cucumber Sandwich Bites

Nutritional Information (Per Serving):

Calories: 90

Carbohydrates: 10g

Protein: 5g

Fiber: 2g

Fat: 3g

Sugar: 3g

Serving Size:

Makes 1 serving.

Prep and Cook Time:

Prep Time: 5 minutes

Cook Time: 0 minutes

Total Time: 5 minutes

Ingredients:

- 1 small cucumber, sliced into rounds

- 2 tbsp cream cheese

- 1 tbsp chopped fresh dill

Instructions:

1. Spread cream cheese on cucumber slices.

2. Sprinkle with dill and serve.

---

16. Protein-Packed Energy Balls

Nutritional Information (Per Serving):

Calories: 180

Protein: 6g

Fat: 8g

Carbohydrates: 20g

Fiber: 4g

Sugar: 8g

Serving Size:

Makes 4 energy balls.

Prep and Cook Time:

Prep Time: 10 minutes

Cook Time: 0 minutes (chilling time: 15 minutes)

Total Time: 25 minutes

Ingredients:

- ½ cup rolled oats

- 2 tbsp almond butter

- 1 tbsp honey
- 1 tbsp chia seeds

Instructions:

1. Mix all ingredients in a bowl until well combined.

2. Form into small balls and refrigerate for 15 minutes before serving.

---

17. Cherry Tomatoes with Mozzarella and Basil

Nutritional Information (Per Serving):

Calories: 150

Carbohydrates: 6g

Protein: 8g

Fiber: 2g

Fat: 10g

Sugar: 3g

Serving Size:

Makes 1 serving.

Prep and Cook Time:

Prep Time: 5 minutes

Total Time: 5 minutes

Cook Time: 0 minutes

Ingredients:

- 1 cup cherry tomatoes
- 1 tbsp balsamic glaze
- ¼ cup mozzarella pearls

Instructions:

1. Combine cherry tomatoes and mozzarella in a bowl.

2. Drizzle with balsamic glaze and serve.

---

18. Avocado Tuna Boats

Nutritional Information (Per Serving):

Calories: 200

Carbohydrates: 8g

Protein: 14g

Fiber: 4g

Fat: 12g

Sugar: 1g

Serving Size:

Makes 1 serving.

Prep and Cook Time:

Prep Time: 5 minutes

Total Time: 5 minutes

Cook Time: 0 minutes

Ingredients:

- ½ avocado

- 1 tsp lemon juice

- 1 small can tuna in water, drained

Instructions:

1. Halve the avocado and remove the pit.

2. Mix tuna with lemon juice and scoop into the avocado halves. Serve immediately.

---

19. Hard-Boiled Egg and Spinach Salad

Nutritional Information (Per Serving):

Calories: 120

Carbohydrates: 4g

Protein: 9g

Fiber: 2g

Fat: 7g

Sugar: 1g

Serving Size:

Makes 1 serving.

Prep and Cook Time:

Prep Time: 5 minutes

Cook Time: 10 minutes (boiling time)

Total Time: 15 minutes

Ingredients:

- 1 hard-boiled egg, sliced
- 1 cup fresh spinach
- 1 tsp olive oil

Instructions:

1. Arrange spinach and egg slices on a plate.
2. Drizzle with olive oil and serve.

---

20. Warm Apple and Cinnamon Bowl

Nutritional Information (Per Serving):

Calories: 140

Protein: 1g

Fat: 4g

Carbohydrates: 26g

Fiber: 4g

Sugar: 18g

Serving Size:

Makes 1 serving.

Prep and Cook Time:

Prep Time: 5 minutes

Cook Time: 5 minutes

Total Time: 10 minutes

Ingredients:

- 1 small apple, diced
- ½ tsp cinnamon
- 1 tsp honey

Emma Grace Stanton

Instructions:

1. Cook diced apple in a skillet over low heat for 3–5 minutes.

2. Sprinkle with cinnamon and drizzle with honey before serving.

Part Four

Beyond the Plate

The Exercise Secret No One Talks About

When it comes to weight loss, most of us have been conditioned to think that endless hours of cardio are the answer. However, while cardio has its place in overall health, relying on it alone is like building a house with only one tool—it simply isn't enough. To truly unlock fat loss and build a resilient, strong body, we need to shift our focus. Strength training, even in short sessions, is the real game-changer.

Why Cardio Alone Will Never Help You Lose Fat

Cardio burns calories in the moment, but its effects stop as soon as you step off the treadmill. Worse, too much cardio can stress your body, raising cortisol levels—a hormone linked to stubborn fat storage, especially around the midsection. On the other hand, strength training creates an "afterburn" effect called EPOC (Excess Post-Exercise Oxygen Consumption). This means your body continues to burn calories long after your workout ends. Even more importantly, building muscle boosts your resting metabolism, allowing you to burn more calories throughout the day without any extra effort.

If you've spent years doing cardio without seeing the results you want, don't worry—it's not your fault. It's simply time to try a smarter approach.

How to Build Lean Muscle at Any Age (in 15 Minutes a Day)

Strength training doesn't have to mean hours in the gym. For women over 50, it's all about efficiency. Short, targeted sessions using body weight, resistance bands, or light dumbbells are incredibly effective. Focus on compound movements—exercises that work multiple muscle groups at once, like squats, push-ups, and rows.

Here's a simple 15-minute routine to get started:

1. **Bodyweight Squats:** 3 sets of 10-12 repetitions.

2. **Wall Push-Ups:** 3 sets of 8-10 repetitions.

3. **Bent-Over Rows with Resistance Bands:** 3 sets of 10 repetitions.

4. **Plank Hold:** 3 rounds of 20-30 seconds each.

These exercises are gentle on your joints but powerful enough to stimulate muscle growth and improve overall strength.

The Most Effective Workouts for Women Over 50

The best workouts combine strength, mobility, and balance. As we age, preserving these elements becomes essential—not just for fat loss, but for maintaining independence and quality of life. Try incorporating functional movements that mimic daily activities, like carrying groceries or climbing stairs. Add light cardio for heart health, but let strength work take center stage.

Strength training doesn't just reshape your body—it reshapes your confidence. As your muscles grow stronger, so will your belief in your ability to tackle challenges both in and out of the gym. This chapter sets the foundation, and in the next, we'll explore how sleep and stress management further amplify your results, proving that true transformation goes far beyond the plate.

Stress, Sleep, and the "Invisible Weight Loss Killers"

It's easy to overlook the hidden factors that sabotage your weight loss goals—stress and poor sleep. These "invisible weight loss killers" don't just slow your progress; they actively work against you. Together, they create a cycle of fatigue, cravings, and hormonal imbalance that makes it nearly impossible to achieve sustainable results. But here's the good news: by addressing these factors, you can supercharge your metabolism and unlock fat-burning potential you didn't know you had.

The Shocking Ways Poor Sleep Is Making You Gain Weight

Sleep isn't just rest; it's a metabolic reset button. When you skimp on sleep, your body's natural rhythms get thrown out of balance. Here's how it works:

- **Increased Hunger Hormones:** Lack of sleep boosts ghrelin, the hormone that makes you feel hungry, and reduces leptin, the hormone that signals fullness.

- **Heightened Cravings:** Sleep deprivation pushes you toward sugary, high-fat foods as your body searches for quick energy.

- **Slowed Metabolism:** A tired body burns fewer calories because it shifts into "conservation mode."

- **Elevated Cortisol Levels:** Poor sleep increases cortisol, which not only stores fat but also breaks down muscle tissue—undoing your hard work at the gym.

Studies show that even one night of poor sleep can impact insulin sensitivity, making it harder for your body to process carbohydrates. Over time, this can lead to stubborn weight gain and increased risk of metabolic disorders.

How to Fall Asleep Faster and Wake Up Refreshed

The key to better sleep is creating an environment and routine that signals your body it's time to rest. Here are some practical tips:

1. **Limit Blue Light Exposure:** Avoid screens at least an hour before bed. Blue light disrupts melatonin production, the hormone that helps you sleep.

2. **Set a Consistent Schedule:** Go to bed and wake up at the same time every day, even on weekends. This trains your body's internal clock.

3. **Create a Relaxing Ritual:** Engage in calming activities like reading, gentle stretching, or meditation before bed.

4. **Control Your Environment:** Keep your bedroom cool, dark, and quiet. A white noise machine or blackout curtains can make a big difference.

Small adjustments like these can drastically improve your sleep quality over time.

The "Sleep Reset Plan" to Supercharge Your Fat-Burning Potential

Think of your "Sleep Reset Plan" as a step-by-step system to optimize rest and boost metabolism:

- **Evening Wind-Down (1 Hour Before Bed):**

  o Turn off devices and dim the lights.

  o Sip on a calming herbal tea, such as chamomile or valerian root.

- **Relaxation Techniques:**

  o Practice 4-7-8 breathing: Inhale for 4 seconds, hold for 7 seconds, exhale for 8 seconds.

Repeat 4-5 times.

- **The First 30 Minutes After Waking Up:**

  o   Get exposure to natural light. Morning sunlight resets your circadian rhythm and improves melatonin production later in the day.

  o   Hydrate with a glass of water to jumpstart your metabolism.

- **Weekends for Recovery:**

  o   Allow yourself an extra hour of sleep if needed, but avoid sleeping in excessively.

What's Next: In the upcoming chapters, we'll explore how to turn these small changes into lifelong habits, ensuring that your efforts are sustainable and rewarding. Remember, better sleep and stress management aren't just about shedding pounds—they're about reclaiming your vitality and feeling like your best self every day.

Part Five

Staying on Track for Life

How to Turn Setbacks Into Comebacks

Setbacks are a natural part of any journey, and your path to better health is no exception. Whether it's a plateau, an indulgent weekend, or an emotional eating episode, these moments don't define your progress—they're opportunities to learn and grow. The key is to approach setbacks with curiosity instead of judgment, turning them into stepping stones for future success.

1. 3-Step Plan to Break Through Weight Plateaus

Plateaus happen when your body adapts to your routine. Instead of feeling stuck, see them as a sign to reassess and refine your approach:

1. **Reassess Your Habits:** Take a closer look at recent changes in your diet, exercise, or sleep. Are portion sizes creeping up? Have workouts become less challenging? Small deviations can stall progress without you realizing it.

2. **Introduce Micro-Adjustments:** Make small, manageable changes. Add 5–10 minutes of strength training, or slightly reduce carb portions on rest days. These minor tweaks can reignite your metabolism without overwhelming your routine.

3. **Cycle Through a Reset Week:** Temporarily return to stricter adherence to the A.D.A.P.T.I.V.E. principles. Adjust meal timing, rebalance macronutrients, and prioritize movement. This reset helps your body recalibrate and pushes past the plateau.

Remember, plateaus are temporary. With these steps, you'll gain momentum and keep moving forward.

2. How to Stop Emotional Eating Before It Starts

Emotional eating is often a response to stress, boredom, or even celebration. Recognizing these triggers is the first step to breaking the cycle.

- **The Pause and Reflect Method:**
  - When you feel the urge to eat, pause for 30 seconds.
  - Ask yourself: "Am I physically hungry, or am I reacting to an emotion?"
  - If it's emotional, identify the underlying feeling—stress, loneliness, or boredom.

- **Alternative Coping Mechanisms:** Replace emotional eating with healthier responses, such as:
  1. Journaling your thoughts.
  2. Taking a short walk.
  3. Sipping a calming tea or practicing deep breathing exercises.

Over time, these practices will help you reframe food as nourishment, not a solution to emotional needs.

3. The Reset Strategy for Overcoming Weekend Indulgences

One indulgent meal doesn't derail your progress—what matters is how you respond. Avoid guilt, which often leads to overcompensation or restrictive behaviors. Instead, focus on balance with a simple **Monday Reset Day Plan**:

- **Hydration First:** Start the day with plenty of water to rehydrate and flush out excess sodium.
- **Prioritize Protein:** Make protein the star of your meals to stabilize blood sugar and curb cravings.
- **Gentle Activity:** Opt for light exercises like yoga or a brisk walk to re-energize.

This plan rebalances your body without extreme measures, helping you reset and move forward with confidence.

Setbacks are not failures—they're opportunities to adjust and refine your journey. The next chapter will guide you on how to solidify these habits, ensuring that the progress you've made becomes the foundation of a vibrant, energized life.

Designing Your New, Energized Life

Reaching your health goals is a significant accomplishment, but maintaining those results and enjoying a vibrant life requires a shift in focus. Rather than staying in "diet mode," this stage is about creating habits that support long-term vitality and joy. By embracing balance and flexibility, you can ensure that your journey feels effortless and empowering.

The 5 Habits That Guarantee Long-Term Results

1. **Consistent Meal Structure:** Build meals with balanced macronutrients—protein, healthy fats, and complex carbs—to sustain energy and prevent cravings.

2. **Regular Strength-Building Exercise:** Aim for 2–3 sessions per week, prioritizing movements that support joint health and muscle maintenance.

3. **Quality Sleep Prioritization:** Protect your rest by sticking to a consistent bedtime routine and ensuring 7–8 hours of sleep. Good sleep is the foundation for energy and recovery.

4. **Stress Management Routines:** Incorporate mindfulness practices like journaling, deep breathing, or short meditations to reduce cortisol and promote mental clarity.

5. **Routine Self-Check-Ins:** Take time weekly to assess how you're feeling physically and emotionally. Adjust your meals, workouts, or rest days as needed to stay aligned with your body's needs.

These habits create a framework that adapts to your lifestyle, making success sustainable and enjoyable.

How to Create a Maintenance Plan That Feels Effortless

Transitioning to "maintenance mode" doesn't mean abandoning structure; it means finding a rhythm that works for you long-term.

- **Sustainable Meal Planning:** Stick to a foundation of healthy choices while allowing room for occasional indulgences without guilt.

- **Workouts You Love:** Shift your mindset from obligation to enjoyment. Find activities that excite you, whether it's yoga, hiking, or dance.

- **Listen to Your Body:** Pay attention to hunger, energy, and satisfaction levels. This intuitive approach prevents over-restriction and supports overall well-being.

Building Confidence and Resilience for a Lifetime of Vitality

True success lies in your mindset. Celebrate non-scale victories, like feeling stronger, more energetic, or confident in your abilities. Accept imperfections as part of life and focus on self-care over perfection.

When discouragement strikes, revisit why you started and seek inspiration in supportive communities or personal growth resources. Remember, your journey is about creating a life that energizes and fulfills you, not one that feels restrictive. This shift in perspective ensures your results are not just lasting but life-enhancing.

Your Personal Success Blueprint

Sustainable progress is built on small, consistent actions. To stay motivated and keep moving forward, it's essential to create a simple system for tracking your achievements, reflecting on challenges, and celebrating wins. This blueprint will help you maintain awareness of your journey and ensure your efforts continue to bring positive, lasting results.

How to Track Progress in 10 Minutes a Week

Tracking doesn't have to be time-consuming or overwhelming. A quick weekly review can provide valuable insights and keep you aligned with your goals. Here's how:

1. **Log Key Metrics:** Spend a few minutes noting your energy levels, workouts, sleep quality, and overall mood.

2. **Focus on Non-Scale Wins:** Look beyond the numbers on the scale. Celebrate strength improvements, reduced cravings, or feeling more confident in your clothes.

3. **Compare and Reflect:** Use this log to identify patterns. For example, notice how better sleep correlates with more productive workouts or fewer sugar cravings.

This process isn't about perfection but awareness. Even small observations can help you make informed adjustments and keep your progress on track.

The 4 Questions to Ask Yourself to Stay Motivated

Reflection is a powerful motivator. Set aside a few moments each week to ask yourself:

- **"What small win am I proud of this week?"** Celebrate even tiny accomplishments, like prepping healthy meals or sticking to a workout routine.

- **"What challenge did I face, and how did I handle it?"** Acknowledge obstacles and give yourself credit for navigating them, even imperfectly.

- **"What will I focus on improving next week?"** Choose one small area to refine, whether it's hydration, meal timing, or stress management.

- **"How am I feeling overall about my journey?"** Check in with your emotions. If you're feeling frustrated, remind yourself why you started and adjust as needed.

Why Celebrating Small Wins Leads to Big Changes

Big transformations are the result of compounded small victories. For instance, drinking more water might seem minor, but over time, it improves digestion, energy, and focus. Reward yourself for these efforts in non-food-based ways, like enjoying a relaxing bath, trying a new fitness class, or investing in gear that supports your journey.

By regularly tracking progress, reflecting on your experiences, and celebrating milestones, you'll stay motivated and empowered to continue creating a life of health and vitality.

Conclusion

Your Journey Is Just Beginning

Congratulations on reaching this point in your journey!

By choosing to read this book, you've already taken an incredible step toward transforming your health and reclaiming your energy. This moment is worth celebrating, not just for the knowledge you've gained but for the commitment you've shown to yourself and your future.

At the heart of this book lies a simple truth: lasting health and vitality aren't about perfection, restrictive diets, or temporary fixes. They're about building sustainable habits, embracing flexibility, and honoring your body's unique needs. Through the A.D.A.P.T.I.V.E. System, you now have the tools to reset your metabolism, balance your hormones, and design a life that energizes and fulfills you—at every stage.

You may still have doubts—about whether you'll stick with these changes, whether setbacks will derail your progress, or whether you're capable of truly transforming your life. Let me reassure you: you are. Progress isn't linear, and challenges are inevitable, but each small step forward builds momentum. Trust in your ability to adapt, learn, and grow. You've already proven you can by making it this far.

So, where do you go from here? Start small. Choose one principle or habit that resonates with you and put it into action today. Whether it's prepping a balanced meal, getting an extra hour of sleep, or reflecting on your weekly wins, every positive choice reinforces your success.

Remember, you are not alone on this journey. Your efforts are part of a larger community of women redefining what health means over 50. Seek out support, share your wins, and continue to learn and grow. There are no limits to what you can achieve when you focus on progress over perfection.

As you move forward, hold onto this: your health is a lifelong gift, and you have the power to nurture it every day.

Leave Your Review!

If this book has resonated with you and helped you take steps toward the vibrant, energized life you deserve, I'd be so grateful if you could share your experience by leaving a review on Amazon.

Your feedback not only helps me understand how this book has impacted you, but it also inspires others to begin their journey with confidence. A few minutes of your time could make a world of difference for someone else looking for hope and a fresh start.

Here are a few simple ways you can make your review even more engaging:

1. **Share Your Story:** Let others know how this book has supported your goals, whether it's a new habit you've embraced, a recipe you loved, or a mindset shift that changed everything.

2. **Include a Photo:** Snap a picture of the cover or a favorite section inside the book. Visuals can inspire others to dive in!

3. **Be Honest and Authentic:** Whether it's a small win or a big transformation, your genuine voice matters.

Just scan the QR code below and you'll be redirected to the amazon review page.

Thank you for taking the time to share your experience. Your review could be the encouragement someone else needs to begin their journey!

Download Your Bonuses!

I'm so excited to offer you even more tools to support your journey! By scanning the QR code below, you'll unlock exclusive bonuses designed to make your progress easier, more enjoyable, and sustainable. Whether it's a 28-day meal plan, quick snack ideas, or additional resources tailored to your goals, these extras are my way of saying thank you for investing in yourself.

Here's how to access your bonuses:

Open your smartphone's camera or QR code scanner app.

Hover over the QR code.

Tap the link that pops up and explore your exclusive content!

Enjoy these resources—you deserve them!

Cooking Measurement chart

Weight

IMPERIAL	METRIC
1/2 oz	15 g
1 oz	29 g
2 oz	57 g
3 oz	85 g
4 oz	113 g
5 oz	141 g
6 oz	170 g
8 oz	227 g
10 oz	283 g
12 oz	340 g
13 oz	369 g
14 oz	397 g
15 oz	425 g
1 lb	453 g

Measurement

CUP	ONCES	MILLILITERS	TABLESPOONS
8 cup	64 oz	1895 ml	128
6 cup	48 oz	1420 ml	96
5 cup	40 oz	1180 ml	80
4 cup	32 oz	960 ml	64
2 cup	16 oz	480 ml	32
1 cup	8 oz	240 ml	16
3/4 cup	6 oz	177 ml	12
2/3 cup	5 oz	158 ml	11
1/2 cup	4 oz	118 ml	8
3/8 cup	3 oz	90 ml	6
1/3 cup	2.5 oz	79 ml	5.5
1/4 cup	2 oz	59 ml	4
1/8 cup	1 oz	30 ml	3
1/16 cup	1/2 oz	15 ml	1

Temperature

FARENHEIT	CELSIUS
100 °F	37 °C
150 °F	65 °C
200 °F	93 °C
250 °F	121 °C
300 °F	150 °C
325 °F	160 °C
350 °F	180 °C
375 °F	190 °C
400 °F	200 °C
425 °F	220 °C
450 °F	230 °C
500 °F	260 °C
525 °F	274 °C
550 °F	288 °C